2007
A POETRY ODYSSEY

After a voya
2,500 years,
has finally r
the stars ...

GW00686349

London
Edited by Michelle Afford

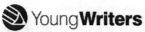 Young**Writers**

First published in Great Britain in 2007 by:
Young Writers
Remus House
Coltsfoot Drive
Peterborough
PE2 9JX
Telephone: 01733 890066
Website: www.youngwriters.co.uk

SB ISBN 978-1 84602 842 7

Foreword

This year, the Young Writers' *2007: A Poetry Odyssey* competition proudly presents a showcase of the best poetic talent selected from thousands of up-and-coming writers nationwide.

Young Writers was established in 1991 to promote the reading and writing of poetry within schools and to the young of today. Our books nurture and inspire confidence in the ability of young writers and provide a snapshot of poems written in schools and at home by budding poets of the future.

The thought, effort, imagination and hard work put into each poem impressed us all and the task of selecting poems was a difficult but nevertheless enjoyable experience.

We hope you are as pleased as we are with the final selection and that you and your family continue to be entertained with *2007: A Poetry Odyssey London* for many years to come.

Contents

Broomfield School

Clapton Girls' Technology College

Connaught School for Girls

Elizabeth Garrett Anderson Girls' School

Geoffrey Chaucer Technology College

Mount Carmel Technology College

Riverston School

St Anne's Catholic High School for Girls, Palmers Green

St Joseph's Academy for Boys, Blackheath

St Joseph's College, Beulah Hill

St Paul's Academy, Wickham Lane

Virgo Fidelis School

Walthamstow School for Girls

William Morris Academy

The Poems

Writing A Poem Is Never Easy!

I am trying to write a classic poem
With a blank page in front of me
It is supposed to be so good
It should make world history.

I have been sitting through time and it's been so long
I have moulded and am stuck to the chair
My thoughts do not form that fabulous song
This is an unfortunate affair!
The bulb has had a fuse
The attic has gone dark
I try to but cannot move
I am malnourished, thirsty and parched.

I can't speak a single word
As my lips are too dry
It is really getting cold
I'm even starting to lose sight.

I am a prisoner in my house
This is a terrible fright
I can't call out
My lungs are squashed and tight.

My tears have made a puddle
On the creaking wooden floor
I can see a slice of light
From the slightly ajar door.

I have lost the battle of will
I resign from the war of life
I head my face towards the sky

With my final breath I free my spirit,
Close my eyes . . .
And whisper goodbye.

Asif Chowdhury (13)

Summer Beauty

Nature calls through the cool air
A spider preparing its web with such care
The green wet grass shines in the morning sun
While girls and boys play with conkers having so much fun.
I hear the wind blow like a whistle
As tiny ripples move through a lake, calm and subtle
A pebble's touch, soft and smooth
Soothing noises vibrate as crickets' legs move.
A flower petal, such a soft touch,
Faint fragrance of lavender, but not much
Trees watching over, big and small
Juicy berries dribbling down your jaw.
Squirrels running up a tree branch
Listen to the crows' chant
As the dogs all bark
You step in mud, leaving marks.
As the leaves wake up by the morning summer breeze
The soft sound of honeybees
An apple tree, large and juicy
Oh how I love summer's beauty.

Chinedu Agwu (12)
Blackheath High School

Desire To Conquer

A hunger for moronic aggression,
Diluted by uncontrollable beads of fear,
Primitive emotions fuelling shivering sensations
That arise upon cool skin.
Whispers of hesitation,
Trapped! Drowned by irrepressible frustrations etched within.
Abrasive tears of anxiety,
Falling, leaves blotches of irate reds upon parched ground.
Silent screams enveloped.
Pent-up aggravations,
Building, increasing, adding to the desire to conquer.

Winifred Ogwang (15)
Blackheath High School

The Dregs

There are those who'll dilly-dally and diddle us
For this, that and a handshake,
Those who'll attack en masse
Wielding knuckle dusters and kebabs,
Those doleful souls who'll badger for a penny
And a 'cup of tea,'
Not least the ones who'll sell religion to you
For a self-proclaimed fantastic price.

There are those, on the other hand,
Who appear to be enthralling,
Those who'll scrounge for their hit of Ritalin or Dieldrin
When not trying their hand at scrawling verse.
Those who'll regularly don their dress suits,
The double basses of the corporate world.
Lastly, those who you'll undoubtedly see,
Those exquisite china dolls,
Their dressage technique perfected
And delicate beauty idolised.

There's a draught these days, a drag,
Devoid of any real romance or charm,
Flummoxing and desultory,
The denouement,
After all, modern times do indeed call for modern people.

Roxie Powell (15)
Blackheath High School

The Dregs

The dregs were disgusting,
The dregs were filth,
They sat in a mug
And murmured like fleas.

The dregs were an abomination,
The dregs were obscene,
The repugnant stench burned
And scathed and stung.

The dregs were humiliating,
The dregs were foul,
People hurled and belched,
As it quilted a blanket of mould.

The dregs were there for months,
Through the damp, the warm, the cold -
Dust gathered on their surface,
Then escaped with the tide of the wind.

The dregs are still neglected,
The dregs are still forlorn,
They still sit in that mug,
They still murmur like fleas.

Rachel Evans (15)
Blackheath High School

A Vibrant Silence

Corridors of stillness, stretching into the deep,
A secretive silence lost in the walls of tranquillity,
Nothing but the lull of a distant heartbeat.

Along the corridor, doors lead to new worlds,
Stepping from nothing to something,
Silence is not hidden behind these panels.
Doors which tempt, doors which don't,
Doors that have not yet been touched
And those which have been gateways many times before.

A door which when opened there is noise behind,
It leads to a different perspective on life,
But even that is quelled by the dark corridor.
This door changes a moment in life,
A moment which is past, present and future,
A moment which is locked away forever.

The mind has a vibrant silence.

Molly Cranston (15)
Blackheath High School

A Disembodied Soul

A disembodied soul
A lost spirit in the night
A forgotten man
A forgotten life
A disembodied soul.

In the endless space
A vibrant silence
The memories of one man
His life replayed
To an audience of no one.

A disembodied voice
Lost within the wind.

Alice Palmer (15)
Blackheath High School

To Break The Heart Of A Lion

To break the heart of a lion . . .
Is like snapping a piece of steel in half.
It is impossible . . .
Or is it not?
A man is like a lion; they act hard and show no emotion,
A real man must not cry, laugh or show sign of frustration.
They are to be proud and walk around their compound
Heads held high,
They look over their family like a lion protects its territory,
They do whatever it takes to achieve the best,
Like a lion does whatever it takes to catch its prey
And yet their hearts cannot be broken,
Men fight to win titles to prove they're number one,
Lions fight to prove they are forever strong
And yet their hearts cannot be broken,
But . . .
Every living thing has a soft spot,
Something that can break them,
A man just needs to experience loss
And a lion to meet another lion with more determination
And your solid steel is turned into shattered glass.

Hannah Chisanga (15)
Blackheath High School

The Proud Heart

I'm the heart that's as thick as stone,
I'm the heart that stands alone,
Where others stand and divide the nation,
I'm the heart that admires the greatest creation.

They lynch with politics, the racists' favourite game,
Segregate and conquer is their plan to keep their shame,
This heart stands strong against discrimination,
Where others stand and divide the nation
I'm the heart that admires the greatest creation.
They seek and demolish those hearts of stone,
Crystal tears shredded from the heart in desperation,
But through every prick it prevails against all odds,
Those hearts of unity struggle to keep themselves profoundly sound,
They struggle to keep that which is being destroyed,
This lonely heart that stands against injustice is indestructible,
This proud heart that stands firm is imperishable.

Ife Edeki (15)
Blackheath High School

Fear Of Failure

A nervousness accompanied by horror
An alarm raised by a phobia
A determination encouraged by desperation A chilling feeling of
Unexplainable fright Holding me captive day and night.
All because of my fear of failure.

Past setbacks and letdowns
Led to my emotional breakdown
Something which is now irreversible
One might say it is my curse to all
Smallest of errors leading to everyone's downfall.
All because of my fear of failure.

Slightest mishaps causing malfunction
Going against tribal rules and customs
These titles I have gained
Due to success I have earned
Having compassion . . . one thing I have not learnt.
All because of my fear of failure.

It's a necessity for me to have some closure
To reveal what is really inside . . .
Would be nothing but exposure
For me to fail would require me to collapse
To hit the ground with nothing but a silent crash.
All because of my fear of failure.

I made my own destiny
Earned my own titles
Tested my own fate
Refused to understand my own history
Prepared my own means of success.

All because of my fear of failure.

Refusing to accept and understand my history
One thing that made the most of me
This catastrophe I have to hide
Using pride to override what is deep inside
For this I will do till the day I die.

All because of my fear of failure.

Nyasha Mafuba (16)
Blackheath High School

Dead Man's Mouth

The dead man's mouth looms now,
His tongue lashing waves of froth,
Devouring my appetite for air,
Unforgotten years cruising,
Between searing-hot sunshine
And glistening azure liquid.

Better to die than live alone,
Discarded, scrap-heaped,
'Too old' for humans to ride,
On my red rusting metal back.
My last journey, their last flight.

I pelt downwards, as swift as an eagle,
Ready to perish in an endless slumber,
Taking hundreds with me,
Into the dead man's mouth.

Renee Campbell (15)
Blackheath High School

My Experience Of War

Every day I can smell
Fire, fear and loss,
The loss of my parents,
The fear of death
And the fire that burns the heart within,
I would die if I could,
But I have a family to live for,
Every day for me gets darker and
Darker,
Slowly . . .

Shahika Ali (13)
Blackheath High School

Village Heartbeat

Hear the voice of the drum,
Tight skin's throaty song,
When the beat wakes with noon's sun,
With the *thrum, thrum, thrum*
And hearts beat in time,
Move with the pulse of the drum,
Can feel something stir,
With the throbbing of the air,
Deep down in everyone,
It's the *thrum, thrum, thrum*.
Starts deep down,
With the shuffle of your feet
And then the fire spreads,
Fills your blood with its heat
And it's caught you up in its clutch,
Can't pause, don't stop,
Mustn't let the beating drop,
The ire-raising, soul-shaking,
Thrum, thrum, thrum.

Caitlin Abbott (15)
Blackheath High School

Patience Beyond Words

It's the same old scene,
You know how it goes,
The one with the 'don't's'
And the 'how should I know's'.
A man and a woman who took it too far,
Their daughter crying in the back of the car.

With the same old excuse, it ends all at once:
'You're scaring her now
And could you just let me out?'
And then of course come the 'Mummy don't go's'
And then the 'don't worry darling, I'm just walking home'.
But how will she know when it really is ending?
At an age where she still thinks you can change
Things by just pretending.
Each time the fights start,
She thinks the time's come,
It might be a relief to live just with her mum.

Clare Fielder (15)
Blackheath High School

The Fear Of Failure

The demons have arrived
They prey on the innocent
Feasting on the brains of the young
Circling around vacant minds of the future
They are there every night and day
And will never go away
They follow you to your dreams, awake or asleep
Till the very day the questions hammer you.

'I want to become a . . . '
'I'll be good at . . . '

Then they strike
Like a thunderstorm on a fragile lamp post
Where has the time gone?
The days draw closer and closer,
As the demons multiply in their pairs.

Soon the presence of the demons is weakened,
The vacant mind clears
And on that very day

Failure is no longer feared.

Maryam Kelani (15)
Blackheath High School

Sad-Faced Youth

As he sat there alone,
He dreamt about the parents he wished he had known,
Occasionally he would gaze at his reflection,
Wondering who he resembled and for a second he
Would feel a connection.
He missed out on the playing, the laughing, and the joking,
He missed out on the bedtime stories, the cuddling and the loving.
He never cried crocodile tears like the other children he knew,
Instead he would cry alone, where he sat, still as stone.
He never had any friends, this sad little boy.
He held a patterned scarf at all times,
Children would point and laugh,
But he was not concerned, as long as he held that scarf,
The scent of her perfume had faded over the years,
Yet still he held it close, to feel free of all fears.

Where has his life disappeared to?
This sad-faced youth.

Emily Briscoe Coleman (15)
Blackheath High School

Follow The Dance

Follow the dance of the bumblebee,
As she waltzes through the sky,
Happy if she's making honey,
Or skimming up high.

Searching for that perfect flower,
With petals of folded silk,
Honey and pollen are special to her,
As to us is Mother's milk!

The sky is dyed a deep red,
Before she heads for home,
Laden down with scented pollen,
To store in honeycomb.

Then she'll fold up her wings of lace
And down her head she'll lay,
To rest in the hive until sunny morning
And a brand new working day.

Daisy Constantine (14)
Blackheath High School

Responsibilities

She walked into the kitchen
The morning fresh and cold
And walked up to the tank
She did what she was told
But as she went to feed it
She noticed something bold
A small orange oval
Floating in the mould.
She crouched down beside it
To see if he was OK
He was alright the other night
What would her parents say?
Would they be annoyed?
They didn't like him anyway.
But suddenly, he began to sink
And lay beneath his bridge
She then began to panic,
Then to think,
I'll hide him in the fridge!
But then she had another thought,
What if he starts to stink?
Then panic grew to anger
And she tugged at her hair
But he was not at all expensive
She'd won him at the fair.
But he was her responsibility
She should have done her job
But he was gone, it wasn't bad
But then she thought of Bob.
Bob was her brother's
The livelier of the two
She saw him in the corner and asked:
'Was this because of you?'
But then she realised the problem,
Bob was dead too.
So she took a bucket and a glove
She knew what she had to do
She opened the lid and rolled up her sleeve
She'd flush them down the loo.

Young Writers - 2007: A Poetry Odyssey London

But why did it happen? What was wrong?
Were they over-fed?
But now it did not matter,
Marley and Bob were dead.

Alice Rose Dean (14)
Blackheath High School

The Echo Of Silence

A time of joy and happiness,
Of hope and love and care,
Was taken sharply away,
From little Johnny Bear.
The tears and the shouting,
The cuts and the bruises,
All were ended abruptly,
By the slam of a wooden door,
The echo of silence ringing out harshly,
Ended by the scream of his mother.
A childhood like no other,
A childhood spent in fear,
An adulthood left in guilt,
There was nothing he could do,
Just look on and pray that one day it would
Stop!

Aoife O'Connor-Massingham (14)
Blackheath High School

Patience Beyond Words

The screams and the shouts
I deal with
The insults, the hurt, the pain,
The tears, the fears,
I'm used to them,
The cuts, the bruises, the shame,
As long as you're near,
I'll deal with it,
To hug me and love me the same,
My daddy, my father,
I'm used to him,
I know that he's not to blame,
The use and abuse,
I deal with
As long as I know you'll be home,
I love you and trust you,
So I'll deal with it,
A patience beyond words.

Hasina Allen (15)
Blackheath High School

A Childhood Lost

No one should be denied the laughter and the smiles,
The gentle stroking of the sunshine on your skin
On carefree summer days,
The love that makes your heart swell and your mouth
Stretch into a grin,
No one should be denied their childhood.
No one should be encouraged to wait for disaster,
Expect it like a friend,
To have a black shadow trace your every move,
To anticipate a war scene upon arrival home,
No one should be denied their childhood.
No one should have losing track of time snatched away from them,
Dragging your feet in sand to make patterns,
Starting a new page,
Laughing so hard you cry,
No one should be denied their childhood.

But she has, she's had it stolen, and now she's been
Left no time to grow,
A lost child lying awake at night listening to the storm rage next door,
Thrown into an adult world, she's lost herself within,
She's been denied her childhood.
A forced referee, she's told to control them,
One weeping in the corner,
The other sitting up in bed shouting things so harsh they hurt to hear,
She's empty inside, an incomplete child, drowned in another body.
It's all too soon, it's all too much, no one can comprehend,
The pain you feel, the confusion you're plagued with,
When you're denied your childhood.

Lois Edmett (14)
Blackheath High School

Superman

Mum and Dad didn't believe me,
They thought it was a lie,
But there he was, Superman!
Flying up so high!
His cloak flying out behind him,
As he soared above my head,
He wasn't good at landing,
For he landed on Dad's shed!
He said only I could see him,
He wanted to be my friend,
To play with and to laugh with,
He would even defend.
We played for hours on end,
Days, weeks, months, years,
But we couldn't stay together always,
As Mum told me our fears.
The first day of school wasn't bad,
I made a new mate,
We laughed together and played
And even made a play date.
As I became closer to my friend,
Superman slipped away,
Now he's soaring in the sky,
Looking for somewhere else to play.
I may have grown up,
For once I was so shy,
But every now and again,
A red cloak catches my eye.

Jodie Kirkland (15)
Blackheath High School

Where Was She?

Where was she when you said your first word,
That word which was as sharp as a sword
And made your father look up to the Lord,
The word which didn't seem to touch him,
But ignited a flame in his eyes?
Where was she when you felt tears clouding your vision,
The pain which seared across your shiny skin,
The hand which felt hot against your raw skin,
The dignity which was lost within?
Where was she when you blew five candles out,
Five candles which went out like a light
And sparked your father to have a fight,
He always knew that he was right,
That you were the one who snuffed her out?

Where was she when your questions were answered in silence,
When your chocolate eyes sparkled with brilliance,
When the tears seemed to go on and on
And you knew that everyone was wrong?
Where was she when you came first
And sliced the air with your fist,
When they placed you on the highest block,
When you wished that something would stop the clock?

Where was she when you studied the night before,
When you thought that you were doomed for sure,
When you fell asleep inside your books
And thought that all teachers were crooks?
Where was she when Hope was born
And your father lifted all his scorn,
When the baby gave its first frown,
But you thought deep down
How happy she would have been,
If she had seen such a little thing?

Amy Smith (14)
Blackheath High School

Sleeping Beauty

It sweeps onto her. Heavy,
Yet light-footed, for it escapes her - unmoved.
She felt it.
The longing looms over her like a pending cloud
Before a storm breaks,
She relaxes as she allows the first shower to wash over her.

She closes her eyes, they are soon sealed,
As the liquid settles, she falls deeper and deeper,
An endless stretch of time blankets her,
Tucked in, a feeling of warmth laps her up,
Vulnerable, she lies, as her soft shell comforts her.
The stories screen through her mind,
She plays her role,
The director: is herself, yet not herself,
She is aware, yet her body lies unmoving, unaware.

Her deepest fears and unborn wishes present themselves
In strange scenes and settings,
People and places are selected and shuffled,
She has the greatest power here,
Under her own spell she believes the illusions.
Only to wake by the spotlight sun
That creeps from the east, beaming,
Or else the drumming raindrops filtering through the
Crack in the windowpane,
Her eyes peel back against the tightening glue,
As she stretches her stiffened body she realises,
She isn't where she thought she was
And things aren't as she believed them to be,
Sighs with relief,
With disappointment,
With anguish.

A smile creeps over her face, contemplating her dream,
The emotions are clear now, the scene is back in place,
Her role is once again, her true self,
Yet the script: unknown.

Zoe Williams (15)
Blackheath High School

Looking Down The Hill

In the shade at the top of the hill,
Looking down on the tall mill,
The grass is growing,
The flowers opening,
All I can smell is dog poo and wee
And I want to climb that tree I see!

Georgia Beswick (12)
Blackheath High School

The Seven Ages Of An Architect

(Inspired by Shakespeare)

Life is a series of crossroads,
But at the end of every one of those many crossroads
Something lies at the end but before you can discover it,
The Seven Ages occur.
First the newborn, wailing and screaming in his mother's arms,
But yelling just to be rocked on his back,
So he can look at the patterns on the ceiling,
After, the toddler wandering around, looking up and around him,
Wondering, *what is that?* And lining up blocks into rows,
Then the schoolboy dragging his feet to school,
But running ahead when he reaches the DT Room.
Knocking blocks together repeatedly until they match,
Then the adolescence, looking up at fine works in museums,
Wondering whether he could achieve such great things,
Then the architect looking down from his open-top roof,
Looking at the fine work he did himself,
Soon to be displayed in The Tate Modern,
At the same time though, aiming higher,
Always looking for the next crossroads,
Knocking the two bricks together but this time - to create a house,
After, when he finishes giving a talk in university,
He looks up at the walls that he built with his own hands
Through his two-inch spectacles,
He reaches the end of the sixth crossroad,
Then when he rocks in his armchair, drooling,
He looks up to the showcase above him
Where awards for his work shimmer,
Although collecting dust
And as he falls into a snooze,
He reaches the end of the last crossroads with the two
Blocks that have been in his hands from when he was born.

Amy Hough (11)
Blackheath High School

Dream

It all fell dark,
He couldn't see, as if blinded by his own imagination,
He felt something brush past his leg like a cat,
He closed his eyes and fell into a silent dream.
The screaming grew louder.
He slipped through space and time
And none could touch or see,
As though the eerie blackness had stolen his soul.

The screaming grew louder.
Why could none see the pain he suffered?
The pain that grew each day,
As each new lie was told,
Each one carved by the hardest of hearts.

The screaming grew louder.
He felt the ground beneath him,
He knows the pain is no more,
He opens his eyes,
He has reached Heaven at last.

The screaming draws to a close
And slowly, slowly,
Stops . . .

Nicola Scott (13)
Blackheath High School

Tiger's Prey

See the tiger, tall and slim,
Waiting for his prey to come,
He hides in the bushes silently,
Staying perfectly still
And then he sees his prey, a deer,
He smiles slightly,
Then jumps out and roars,
The deer starts to run,
But the tiger's too fast,
Within seconds the deer is dead,
The tiger's family for tonight is fed.

Anne-Marie Sewell (11)
Blackheath High School

Cats

They always know how to cheer you up when you're down,
Making you smile.
They always let you know when they're in the room,
Making you laugh.
Every day they will ask you to stroke them,
Making you feel wanted.
Most of the time they know when you want to be alone,
Making you feel understood.
And every cat has a secret way of knowing
When you want them,
Making you feel special!

Beatrice Paterson-Achenbach (11)
Blackheath High School

I Saw A Snail

I saw a snail.
It was sliding across
The path in front of me,
Leaving a trail of slime.
It was ugly,
It was slow,
So easy to crush . . .

I'm so cool and unique.
No one else can carry their house
On their back.
I'm strong,
I'm tough,
No one would ever try to take me on . . .

Should I crush it?

Lata Nobes (11)
Blackheath High School

Elephants

You see them plodding along slowly,
The elephants in the zoo,
Why do they look so sad?
Is it right to shut them away?
Shouldn't they be wild?
Everyone looking straight at them,
Wouldn't you get annoyed?

Emma Falk (11)
Blackheath High School

Moving On

When I lived with you I took you for granted,
You were the person with whom I was planted,
You were there for me through good times and bad,
You comforted me when I was sad,
Then I moved out and everything changed,
The small world I knew became large and strange,
The room I was given was dirty and cold,
I wasn't myself, I was timid not bold,
The people around me all knew what to do,
They didn't care, I was just someone new,
I became so forgetful, I lost all my books,
I was afraid of the teachers, I was afraid of their looks,
All the food that I ate was just burgers and chips,
I longed for some of your organic dips,
The novels I had to read were so incredibly long,
When I did my test I found my answers all wrong,
One gloomy old Saturday I couldn't take it anymore,
I felt like having a tantrum, kicking and screaming on the floor!
Luckily I contained my anger like you taught me to,
I looked for a smart idea, a start that was good as new,
The funny thing was I got higher levels,
To me the teachers seemed less like devils,
Finally it was the holidays, oh hip hip hooray!
When I arrived home, I didn't know what to say,
You were there with Dad and Jake
And behind you was a *huge* sponge cake,
There were presents and cards and flowers as well,
Then guess who arrived, my old best friend Mel.
I was so overwhelmed, I began to cry,
But all the happiness was over in a whoosh and a fly,
So here I am sitting glumly on the train,
Waiting for the good times and the bad times to roll over again.

Buffy Eldridge-Thomas (11)
Blackheath High School

The Lonely Polar Bear

Do you really care,
For the big polar bear?
Well if you do then why do you
Keep the light on at night,
So you can sleep tight?
Don't keep the TV on standby,
You will make the polar bear cry.
Don't take the car,
If you don't have to go far.
So do you really care for
The big polar bear?

Lara Laeverenz-Schlögelhofer (11)
Blackheath High School

To Break A Lion's Heart

Only one thing would break this lion's heart,
Being like his father would tear him apart,
Strong and bold yet so fearful of something mild,
Having taunted him from a child,
Agbala was the name for a man unknown,
He didn't want to be this, sad, alone,
Having to work for everything he's got,
Being everything his father is not.

Courtney Brown (15)
Blackheath High School

My Corner

I am sitting in my corner watching the world go by,
Wondering where it all went,
I watch the wind dance with the leaves,
Teasing them with its power and might,
The way that I used to play with my siblings.

I listen to the melody of a sweet songbird,
As it sings with all its heart and might without a care in the world,
Oh, how I wish I could be free,
Free of the responsibilities of life.
I smell the blossoming flowers, a smell that comes once a year,
So sweet and fresh,
A smell of newborn youth,
Youth that is slipping through my fingers,
Something so untouchable.

I hear the creaking of a long-forgotten swing,
A new home for spiders and other things, It was once a swing loved,
But it is now forgotten.
I walk to my window
And breathe in fresh air around me,
I put a mental lock on all,
That I once cared for.

My mum whispered into my ear,
'You will always be my little girl,
With black curly hair.'

Kimberley Burton-Lynch (14)
Blackheath High School

Darkness

It's nearly time to go to bed,
All these thoughts whirling through my head,
My imagination expanding,
About the googlies on the landing.
I have these rituals you see,
It starts by counting 1, 2, 3,
Then I stand and steer,
Hoping the shadows disappear.

I check the wardrobe, under the chair,
Under my bed to banish my fear,
Then I slowly climb up in my bed,
Pull the cover over my head.

Just my eyes peeking out,
'Lights out,' I hear my mum shout,
Then the room is plunged in darkness,
Shadows creaking,
Branches knocking on the window like witches' fingers.

Luckily I have had a long day,
So sleepiness is on its way.

Lauren Martin (14)
Blackheath High School

The Snow Lion

Lions live in Africa or so I'd always read,
Where sun beats down on dusty plains
And skies are burning red,
But our lion lived near Harrogate,
Out on a Yorkshire dale,
He wasn't made of warm brown fur
And had no fluffy tail.
To us it was the best lion,
That we had ever seen.
We made it with our mitten hands,
We built it as a team.
Oh, it was cold, the icy winds
Blew through my winter hat,
But we didn't seem to notice,
Building our icy cat.
Its mane of twigs,
Its eyes of coal
And body made of snow,
We played on it for hours,
We didn't want to go.
For the whole time we were there,
We talked to our new friend.
He had a name, Snowsimba
And to his needs we'd tend.

Then one day we went outside,
The sun was shining bright
And Snowsimba, well he'd gone away,
He must have left that night.

We all trudged inside sadly,
Then something caught my eye.
A cloud shaped like Snowsimba
Was scudding through the sky.
'He's melted,' said my cousin Nick,
But he just didn't know,
Snowsimba had gone flying,
To find some fresh, new snow.

Anna Beketov (14)
Blackheath High School

My Rosie

Her name was Rosie,
She was my best friend.

A great listener
And always there to defend.

She had the prettiest dresses
And the shiniest hair.

The nicest parents
And the coolest au pair.

We played together every summer
And made up loads of games.

She helped me with my reading
And also with my aims.

We went out playing
And the worst thing came about.

My Rosie.
Her arm fell out.

Rebecca Stewart (14)
Blackheath High School

Childhood

I sat in my rocking chair,
Feeling a breeze on my cheek, so bare,
Like an angel sighing, so gentle and meek,
I wanted nothing more than to sit and weep.
I watched them playing,
Laughing and saying,
Singing like nightingales,
With added shouts and wails.

'Look at me! Look how I've grown!'
'I'm taller than the trees!' I heard one moan,
'No, you're not!' I heard another tease,
I laughed with an edge of wheeze.
I sighed and reached for my old friend Shaun,
His fur so coarse and oh so torn,
He's been with me from start till end
And he's never been short of a friend.

I heard the patter of little feet,
I let my eyes flutter and meet,
Their cheerful faces, glowing with youth,
Unlike mine so old, cold, that's the truth.

If I could turn back time,
I'd go back to when life was fine,
When I was dazzled by the wonders of childhood,
Oh, if only I could.

Lillie Gredley (14)
Blackheath High School

Hearing Children Laughing

I heard the children laughing,
I watched the children play,
I saw the parents smiling,
On that warm and sunny day.

But one boy he wasn't grinning,
Just sitting on his own,
Tentatively binning,
A piece of paper with a groan.

I heard the children laughing,
As I watched them stand in line,
I saw the races starting,
On this day so bright and fine.

But the boy he would not run,
He just frowned and shook his head,
He didn't see the fun,
He would rather wait instead.

But his mother never came,
He wanted to go home,
It was always the same,
He was forgotten and alone.

I heard no children laughing,
I watched the fading light,
I saw the small boy crying,
On this cold and empty night.

Sarah Punter (14)
Blackheath High School

Nature

Walking through the park one day,
Wondering why God made it this way,
Warm breeze hitting my face,
Whilst I moved from place to place.

As the birds sang sweetly in the trees,
How wonderful, it seemed to be so free,
As the clouds moved through the beautiful blue sky,
A magnificent magpie caught my eye.
How lovely and green was the grass,
I just didn't want this moment to pass,
As the clear, fresh water sprouted from the fountain,
It was so high it looked like a mountain.

Squirrels darted here and there
And conkers lay everywhere,
As we walked back to school,
I was thinking *that was cool.*

The wonderful, beautiful, magnificent nature,
Oh how I would love to meet the maker.

Kayisha Payne (12)
Blackheath High School

Journey Through The Park

The grass was full of dew,
That bounced up your leg,
The sky splodged with clouds,
With sunrays burning upon your head.

The flowers' colourful buds opened,
Sending out that pollen smell,
With shadows shading the deep emerald grass,
Where the creatures played upon the ground.

The wind blew into your face,
Your feet squelched in the dirty mud,
The birds sang a melodic tune,
While they soared around above.

The conkers fell from the trees,
Where they lay waiting to be picked,
Surrounded by brightly coloured berries,
Until noisy humans came and they got kicked.

Remziye Toprak (12)
Blackheath High School

Four Or Five

When I was about four or five,
I was a short and chubby girl,
Whenever my mum's friends came along,
The first thing they did was pull my cheeks,
Then they would want to pick me up,
Swinging me as if I were a baby.

When I was about four or five,
I laughed and also cried a lot,
I always stamped my feet when I cried,
I cried every day and everywhere,
I would cry if I can't buy toys,
I would cry when I couldn't find my mum.

When I was about four or five,
I would throw all my toys out,
But I would never tidy them up,
I would take them everywhere with me,
But I would drop one occasionally,
Every time I dropped one,
My mum had to buy me a new one.

Cheryl Lee (14)
Blackheath High School

That Time In Your Life

You will always remember that time in your life
The important start to your journey,
Stumbling and tripping along the way
And learning many things,
There were friends and family to help you along,
To give you a gentle hand,
To comfort you when you were feeling low,
To protect and keep you safe.

You will always remember that time in your life,
'Ready or not - here I come!'
Is the call you hear across the playground,
Footsteps come creeping closer,
Closer to your hiding place,
You tremble and hold your breath . . .
Crunch, you freeze fast with fear and exhilaration,
'Boo! I found you!'

You will always remember that time in your life
When you had a wild imagination,
Invisible friends, unicorns and fairies,
All living in your house,
Running and jumping onto your bed,
To escape the savage snatch of the beasts,
Placing your tooth under your pillow,
For the tiny tooth fairy to collect while you dream.

You will always remember that time in your life,
When you were wide-eyed and small,
You will always treasure the experiences you had,
As you grew into becoming *you!*

Hannah Laeverenz-Schlögelhofer (14)
Blackheath High School

Change

Past days forgotten,
When I was young,
Things were so different,
So much more fun.

Innocence I had
And that I hope to keep,
Missing the life I once had,
Alive only in my sleep.

Playing in the garden,
With childhood bliss,
Talking with the friends,
Who I've come to miss.

Today nothing is a joke,
Serious all the time,
Bad influence in corners,
Me, far from fine.

Missing the way it used to be,
Friendships with my family,
The love I had for my friends,
The beauty I saw in making amends.

Childhood bliss I've come to miss.

Athena Rayburn (15)
Blackheath High School

Charlie

No one believes me about my friend Charlie,
What he does and where he goes,
Everyone thinks that I'm responsible,
But I'm not, I'm really not,
He leaves messages in the dark,
Secrets only I will understand
And the very first time I met him,
He showed me exactly
What he was capable of.

Our favourite game was hide-and-seek,
Charlie always hid,
He never failed to leave me clues
And I never failed to find them,
But these clues weren't the ordinary,
An upturned corner of a duvet,
Or the creaking of wooden floor,
These clues were something special,
A warning, to all.

Because in the pitch-black darkness,
That's where Charlie is,
He's waiting for his next victim,
Silent, secretive,
He doesn't mean to do it,
But it's just the way he lives,
His clue,
A trail of blood,
That never stops shining.

Emma Creed (14)
Blackheath High School

How It Used To Be . . .

Sitting on a carpet,
In a room full of kids,
Laughing with the teacher,
That's how it used to be . . .

Sitting on the 'silly bench',
When you have been told off,
Getting sent home,
When you have got a cough.

Calling teachers by their first names,
Wearing our own clothes,
That was the life in Prior Weston,
That's how it used to be . . .

Playing football with the boys,
Gossiping with my friends,
Playing 'tag' around the school,
Why did it all have to end?

Georgia Arron-Unsworth (14)
Blackheath High School

Stop Bullying Me

Every day, as I walk to school,
Bullies laughing, thinking they're cool,
I hang my head, a tear from my eye,
My friend runs up to me, 'There's no need to cry.'

Our first lesson is PE,
I can't do it, I've scraped my knee,
The bullies say I am a baby,
I don't want to do it, but they practically make me.

Out we go into the playground,
My head spinning round and round,
The captains have to pick teams first,
Of course I am last, I am going to cry, I am going to burst.

I get pushed and shoved,
My bracelet snaps, the one I love,
They laugh, they titter,
They drop lots of litter.

The teacher sighs,
Says I'm telling lies,
He says, 'Pick up all the rubbish!'
He adds to that, 'And sharpish!'

The bullies shout and tell me to go home,
They say I will never have friends, I'll always be alone,
One of them says, 'Go on, go!'
I can't take it, I scream and shout, I say, 'No!'

They all get scared, they run away,
They'll never bully me again, not any day,
I feel so happy, the dark turns to light,
I never have to be scared again,
I'll never have to fight.

Diksha Shah (11)
Broomfield School

Launch

Land engulfed in smoke,
Air left torched and bare,
That is the price for discovery,
But discovery is a gleaming prospect,
Especially when you leave the Earth behind,
For a faraway planet or moon . . .

Lyle Holloway (12)
Broomfield School

The 10 O'Clock News

Think about the Third World
And all those little boys and girls.

Who are unable to learn,
Instead, with harsh jobs they earn.

As I lay warm in bed at night,
I think how they're denied the right.

To play and embrace life like a child,
Discover the world, its places and act wild.

Why do we not realise how lucky we are?
Imagine living there, if not working, we starve.

Farhana Begum (12)
Broomfield School

My Parents

Some parents are mature,
Some parents are childish.

My parents are crazy,
Sometimes they can be lazy.

My mum is like a baby,
Who needs to be cared for with special help.

My dad takes the mick,
When people try to be strict.

Together they are worse,
Because they are united of course.

This is my story about my parents,
Just be grateful you ain't me!

Alisha Ahmed (12)
Broomfield School

You'll Make It Through

You know those days when you feel sad,
Ticked off, somewhat mad,
Or maybe just tired of the pain.

I sometimes feel the same,
Weary of this game,
The one they call life.

Ever since day one,
Life hasn't been too much fun,
Living like it's a punishment,
Friends come and go,
What do we really know?

But I can tell you one thing,
Although life has dragged you down
And placed you like a fool,
Love will get you through
And happiness will find you,
Whatever the cost, I'll stand by you.

Promise . . .

Samia Arbad (14)
Broomfield School

The Daisy

There is stands, alone in the field,
The sweet melody can be heard from the newly born birds,
There it stands, alone, independent and worthy of its own,
There it stands, swaying with the gentle breeze,
The bees dare not collect the contents in the middle,
For they know it's wrong,
There it stands with beauty and grace,
Not even an angel could compare,
It is the daisy, the one who survives storms,
There the lonely daisy once stood.

Lydia Singh (12)
Broomfield School

Identity

Identity,
What is identity?
Identity is about:
Who you are,
What you are,
And where you are,
Bengali, Pakistan, Japanese or a Christian,
Be happy with who you are,
We are all God's creations,
We are all beautiful in our own way,
We are all unique,
You don't have to be Angelina Jolie to be beautiful,
Just be yourself,
Even personality counts,
Be kind, be rude, be helpful, be lazy,
Just have a good heart,
Religion,
We are all from different cultures which makes us special,
I'm Noori Amina,
I am Muslim,
Yet I live in England,
Bonding with others,
I play, I pray, that's what I say,
Yet I celebrate Eid, I fast during the month of Ramadan
And that's my identity,
What's yours?
Whoever you are,
Wherever you are,
Just be happy with who you are,
Remember it's what is in your heart that counts,
Nothing else.

Noori Amina (12)
Clapton Girls' Technology College

Equality

What does equality mean?
Equality means,

Everyone is special,
Different in their own way,
Everyone's laughing, happy to play,
When each of us is born,
There are celebrations,
No matter what race you are,
No matter if you've come from afar,
Black, white or mixed race,
We're all the same,
Even if one of us has fame,
We're all equals to each other,
All of our dreams have no limitations,
The only things different are,
Our names,
Our religions,
Our qualities,
Our personality,
Our ethnicity,
Our backgrounds,
Our hair,
Our skin texture,
Our eyes,
Our body shape,
Our voice,
Our handwriting,
Our habits,
Our thoughts.

Sulekha Jama (13)
Clapton Girls' Technology College

Identity

I found a letter on the side, titled, 'Expressions of a Person Inside,'
I opened and found words of a heart being poured,
Soulful words and touching lines, were written on the
                              letter as words of fine.

Lonely and ravishing, beautiful to see,
But unfortunately, she really hated me,
But perhaps that was my own fault,
Shocked, by the words I saw, but decided to carry on,
Cute and adorable, whenever with an angry face,
But always in a hurry, rushing without leaving a trace.

Caring and responsible, helping people's needs,
Always on the lookout, erupting good deeds,
Trustworthy and reliable, with secrets buried in her heart,
Intelligent and gentle, also very smart.

As I read on, I slowly started to understand this person's words,
And kept on reading,
Cute and generous, always acting sweet,
But I was heartbroken when I found out we could never meet.

Persuasive and bay like and sometimes a bit mean,
But never intentionally would be hurtfully keen,
Sometimes quite funny, sometimes quite loud,
But would never want to embarrass anyone in front of any crowd.

I started to realise it wasn't any sort of letter,
But actually was meant for someone and had a meaning,
Inside of it, but I still forced myself to read on.

It wasn't because of the hatred she had against me,
It's just the happiness on her face that I wanted to see,
But now I've decided to give up on all my hopes
And dedicate my entire life to her, but will she?

After reading it, I was left without any words, but then,
I walked down to the bottom of the letter and saw a girl's name
And when I saw it, I was completely broken,
It was actually my name that was written.

Mozufa Begum (13)
Clapton Girls' Technology College

Identity

No matter where you come from,
England, Ghana, Israel,
We all have one thing in common,
We are people of this world,
Our souls,
Like fingerprints, are never the same,
But we can all be identified,
By our name,
I am only young
And maybe not one to talk,
But we could all unite
And walk the walk,
But then,
Why are there gunshots, violence and crime?
I guess this is a question that can only be solved with time,
I come from Ghana,
You may too,
The land of gold,
Though now there is few,
Of my grandparents, I do not know,
Though I hope, for you, that this ain't so,
The hand of friendship has no colour,
Mixed race, white, black, blue,
On the inside,
There is no difference,
Between me and you,
I hope you listened carefully
And will apply this to your life,
I know I will,
To the day I die.

Susan Yakuba (13)
Clapton Girls' Technology College

Identity

Me,
My style, my life,
My attitude, my sign,
My culture, my language,
Me,
I was born to cry,
I was born to laugh,
I was born to be cute,
I was born to have a life,
Me,
Sometimes I'm good,
Sometimes I'm bad,
Sometimes I'm rude,
Sometimes I'm fab,
No one can stop me being
Who I am,
Me,
I have learnt to speak,
I have learnt to write,
I have leant to read,
I have learnt to fight,
Me,
I've got my style,
I've got my attitude,
I've got my right,
I've got my life,
Me,
Everyone is equal, no matter what,
So be proud like me,
Of your identity!

Sibel Halibryam (13)
Clapton Girls' Technology College

The World

Why can't there be peace in the world?
Why can't people be equal?
Why do we have war?
Can't there be peace in the world?
People are suffering when it is not their fault,
People are crying because they don't have love,
Why can't there be peace in the world?
Children are on the streets,
Waiting for someone to help them,
Children are working day and night
Because they don't have a home to go to,
Why can't there be peace in the world?
It does not matter what race you are or what you believe,
It does not matter what language you speak or
What colour you are,
Everyone is equal, so why can't there be peace in the world?
Why is there crime and all sorts of violence in this world?
Why do we use all sorts of weapons?
Why can't we make it all stop?
Why can't there be peace in the world?
Think before you do something,
Think before you speak,
Think of how people will feel if you do something to upset them,
So make it *all stop!*
And make this world a better place
By spreading *peace!*

Farzana Patel (13)
Clapton Girls' Technology College

Ha, Ha, He, He, Ho, Ho, Ho

Ha, ha, he, he, ho, ho, ho,
That's my laugh and I know it's funny,
But please don't laugh,
Don't be like the others,
Because when I laugh like that,
Ha, ha, he, he, ho, ho, ho,
People stare at me and laugh
And this sets me off into a fit of giggles,
Trust me, it sounds like alien language
When I talk so fast and so much,
Ha, ha, he, he, ho, ho, ho,
It doesn't matter where I am, school, shops, clubs or home,
It's as if the entire world has the knowledge of my funny laugh,
Ha, ha, he, he, ho, ho, ho,
People know I'm ashamed of it because I burn up
                              and get rosy cheeks,
But I can't help it!
If I could, don't you think I would have done so?
Ha, ha, he, he, ho, ho, ho,
I'm a loud person by nature,
It's just who I am,
But when that laugh stirs up in me,
It echoes through my head to my ears,
As I sit there, stand there, embarrassed,
Looking at the laughs around me,
It changes me and makes me feel coldly alone,
Ha, ha, he, he, ho, ho, ho,

So please don't laugh at me,
I've come here to try,
I want a life, a nice one
And I want you to be part of it, to help me,
My last hope, my last chance,
My last laugh,
Ha, ha, he, he, ho, ho, ho.

Summaiya Undre (14)
Connaught School for Girls

The Dove Of Love

A gentle twinkle in Cupid's mind,
Marks the start of a story ranging through all time,
So listen carefully line by line
And spread the story that's no longer mine.

Rough is the roaring sea God's temper,
As she gently soothes his burning rage,
With her cold calm touch, softer than the feathers Egyptians weighed,
But this time she can fight no longer,
The love is back but this time stronger,
His love now made fonder,
Must find a home,
In a heart that is now a stone.

Now she floats alone,
Desperately feeling the pain,
Of Cupid's aim, that she swears will turn her insane,
So now she begs, they beg, he begs,
'Take your wretched love, stupid Cupid,
For my heart's not to be bound, it's free like a dove.'
People beg night and day,
Though they no longer can tell the difference they say,
'Give us back the sun we crave,
Set us free from the grey, that grey that plagues our every day,'
Her love begs day and night,
'Share with me the burden of love in all its might,
For you are the wind not to be bound to me,
Instead to be united and together roam free,
With me, the sea.'

No longer could she bear the burden of denial,
Or fight brave destiny in that style,
So with the release of the white doves of peace,
Did her ongoing pain suddenly cease.

Suddenly, the quilt of grey was lifted, with the people's dismay,
Leaving no reason for Neptune to have to pray,
So now we see the reason why,
True love is our only ally,
For to fight it you will only cause grief,
But alight it and unite with it and life will reach peaks,
Beyond human belief.

Jaccaidi Hypolite-Dyer (14)
Connaught School for Girls

Imprisoned From Nature

I stepped out into the garden as if for the first time,
The bright sun blinding my eyes, and forcing me to look away,
I breathed in the fresh spring air, letting it into my lungs,
I savoured the sweet taste of heat on my tongue,
I looked around me and at the amazing sights that filled the garden,
I saw a bird not far away, perched on a nearby fence,
It landed as light as a feather, on a nearby tree,
I caught sight of a bee buzzing towards a flower,
I watched as it stopped and carried onto the next,
I heard the rustle of a leaf as it fell from a tree,
Knowing it would be replaced by another,
I watched as the world came to life around me,
I watched and realised that the world had changed,
The world had moved on, while I had spent my life in prison,
Life had moved on, while mine had frozen,
I looked around myself and at the things I'd been restricted from
And as I did, I realised what had happened to me,
I had been imprisoned from nature,
I had been someone who hadn't seen the break of daylight for years,
I had been someone who hadn't seen a living thing
                              for months on end,
I had been someone whose life was left in ruins,
I had been imprisoned from nature,
But now I had seen the flight of a bird,
I had seen a bee pollinate a flower,
I had heard the rustle of a leaf,
I had experienced the power of nature,
I had been imprisoned from nature . . .
But now I was free.

Khadeejah Undre (13)
Connaught School for Girls

Friendship

Friends are everlasting,
Even when they are fasting,
They will last me forever,
They will leave me never,
Cheer me up when I am sad,
Make me laugh, when I act mad,
Help me with my issues,
When I am ill, they give me tissues,
Never ever lie,
Always say 'Hi'
Invite me round to their house,
Even if I act like a mouse,
Truthful they are,
But not too far,
Always there for you
And you're there for them too.

Razina Patel (11)
Connaught School for Girls

Cliffhanger

I was gazing at the breathtaking surroundings,
The jagged cliffs opposite me,
The rushing waterfall cascading down below me,
The works of nature in action.

I could taste,
The citrus fruits dispersing their flavours,
The soft breeze entering in my mouth,
The works of nature in action.

I could hear,
The beautiful song of the nightingale,
The whispering of the evergreen trees,
The works of nature in action.

I could smell,
The perfume of a blooming rose,
The scent of freshly cut grass,
The works of nature in action.

I could feel,
The wind rustling through my hair,
The blood rushing to my head,
The works of nature in action.

I was hanging off a cliff,
Hanging upside down,
Gazing at the works of nature,
Lying before my eyes.

Racha Sobratee (12)
Connaught School for Girls

Second Best

It's been a long time,
But I shall never forget,
You live on and live your dreams,
Die but rest in peace,
But never forget,
The dancer you left,
Behind,
Do your Broadway shows
And run your dance rehearsals,
But never forget the dancer,
You left out in the cold, blizzard and snow,
Hope your career prospers
And blooms like a flower,
But never forget
The dancer,
Who wasn't good enough,
To follow in your footsteps,
Live on and live your dreams,
But never forget the dancer you left,
Behind
From second best.

Claudia Biriwaah-Yeboah (12)
Connaught School for Girls

Why?

Why do we live in fear?
Why are our eyes filled with tears?
Judged by the clothes we wear,
When we are getting battered, why don't they care?

Why do they hold a knife,
Hoping to take another life?
Why are we living in strife?
Do they think this makes the world nice?

Bang!
They've shot another one,
The young girl is just still, dying,
While her mother is by her side, crying.

Why does the smallest thing cause the biggest fights?
Why can't they stop and get things right?

Why is the question whose answer no one can find,
Why is the only word on my mind.

Chika Ugboaja (12)
Connaught School for Girls

Witch's Spell

Eye of lizard, toe of frog,
Tail from rat, and bark from dog,
Sneeze of chicken, cough of bat,
Lick of weasel, smell from cat.

Stir it up, mix it well,
To make a marvellous monster spell.

Leeches' livers, finely chopped,
Plus a pimple, freshly popped,
Web of spider, a slimy toad,
Remains of hedgehog, scraped from the road.

Stir it up, mix it well,
To make a marvellous monster spell.

The spell has gone wrong,
Oh no! The monster is from Hong Kong.

She grabs her wand, she has a notion,
Of how to get rid of this potion.

She shakes her wand, which breaks the spell
And waves the monster a fond farewell.

Heena Bux (11)
Connaught School for Girls

My Mistake

As I walked down this lonesome stairway,
Trying to get to the light, day after day,
It is now I realise the time that has been wasted,
Oh those memories of which I wished to have tasted,
I thought pride was everything,
Too embarrassed to cry, too embarrassed to sing,
Every time I looked at you, you went all red,
You were the fragrance of a flower bed,
What is the point of remembering this now?
To me life was 'Wow!'
Don't make the same mistakes I did,
Don't slip down the same slide I did,
Don't remember me now,
It's the light I see,
It's not the light you see.

Sanya Ahmed (13)
Connaught School for Girls

Unfinished Goal

I might as well take a knife
And stick it through my soul
As living this life is utterly worthless
With this unfinished goal.
I'm not alive, nor am I dead,
In-between both worlds,
Trying to end my life at last,
Because I'm worth no more than gold,
I'm living with my loneliness,
Slowly struggling through,
Trying to get through loneliness,
Without the love from you.
Now I hope you're living life,
The way you wanted to,
Without me there to stop your ways,
That's my prayer to you,
You wonder what the goal is,
So I think I should tell you,
That my aim in life, which I didn't complete
Was to actually love you.
I couldn't do this, as you know,
You hurt me day and night,
So when I slept next to you,
I held my dead heart tight,
I make the slit just above my heart,
Before the morning lights
And so, with this note, I finally tell you,
I hope you sleep well tonight.

Charlotte Cole (12)
Connaught School for Girls

Bullying

I feel lonely,
I feel trapped,
Every horrible thing you say to me,
Makes me feel like you're putting a dagger through my heart,
Have you ever heard of 'sticks and stones may break my bones,
But words will never hurt me'?
Oh how wrong they are,
I feel like a tiny grain in a huge meadow,
Do I wish I was dead?
No, because that would make my bullies happy,
I hate school, I hate the world,
This could all be dealt with, with one sharp knife.

Jamilla Bruce (12)
Connaught School for Girls

People Dying, People Crying

People dying, people crying,
Different races, different cases,
We need to know we all go at different paces,
No more fights,
No more bites,
Everyone's in the pace,
All the same case,
At one race,
The human race!
People laughing, people smiling,
Together we unite,
In this one special night,
Helping each other fly a kite,
People laughing, people smiling,
Everyone's trying,
Everyone's crying,
The cry of happiness,
People and their kindness,
Together we stand,
Believing that together we can
Now all that's left is,
People laughing, people crying,
I wish!

Sara Patel (14)
Connaught School for Girls

Sizes

So what if I am tall? I can look over all,
I can see things, I can reach things, but can you?
I can get on rides for people tall enough,
I can get into older films but can you?

So what if I am small? I can fit in little things,
I can hide well in hide-and-seek,
I could grow, but can you?

So what if I am fat? I can be noticed,
I can be different but can you?
I can be free, I can shake my booty but can you?

So what if I am skinny? I can run faster than you,
I am more flexible, I can fit in all styles,
I can bend and stretch,
I can be different but can you?

So what if we are all different sizes?
People come in different sizes,
We are created equally so be happy,
Some people wish to be skinnier,
Some people wish they could put on weight,
Some want to be taller or smaller,
So please appreciate!

Felicia Davies (14)
Connaught School for Girls

God Give Me A Second Chance

Pale and weak, she is so small,
There is no cry, she does not call,
Her eyes don't open, they stay glued shut,
I'm hoping and praying for God to give her luck.

So quickly she is taken away,
Not just for hours but for many days,
Lying in her life-saving cage,
I sit by her side; I'm in an everlasting daze.

One quiet night there's an awakening noise,
Beep, beep the machines call,
The doctors and nurses come running in,
I feel like I'm drowning, I cannot swim.

I remember that night so very well,
Every so often my eyes begin to swell,
I thank God with all my heart,
That he has given me a second chance.

Tonight I sit by the small single bed
And stroke my little girl's soft head,
She is happy and so am I,
Because she did not die, neither did I.

Hannah Amartey (16)
Connaught School for Girls

When You're Strong Enough To . . .

When you're strong enough to stand up for what you believe in,
When you're strong enough to rule the world,
When you're strong enough to use your brains not your fist,
When you're strong enough to let your wings unfold.

When you're strong enough to experience love and pain,
When you're strong enough to know life is a game,
When you're strong enough to take triumph and disaster
And not separate the two,
When you're strong enough to learn the sky really isn't blue.

When you're strong enough to be able to say no,
When you're strong enough to handle the truth,
When you're strong enough to be responsible for your actions
And understand not everything is true.

When you're strong enough . . .
Only then will you realise, it all lies in you.

Faiza Mohamed (15)
Connaught School for Girls

Friendship

You're a true friend,
That I want you to know,
Our love for each other,
Has helped us to grow.

We've been through some tough times,
But we've made it through,
The only one I ever trusted was you.

You helped me through anger,
You've chased away my tears,
You held me through sadness
And rubbed away my tears.

You stayed by my side,
When the world turned away,
You helped me see joy,
When the skies were all grey.

Saima Hussain (11)
Connaught School for Girls

Friendship

A friend is someone we turn to,
When our spirits need a life,
A friend is someone we treasure,
For friendship is a gift,
A friend is someone who fills our lives,
With beauty, joy and grace
And makes the world we live in,
A better and happier place.

A friend is someone who treats you,
The opposite of the way you think they would,
A friend is someone who lets you hold on to them,
When you're afraid of something they're not,
A friend is someone who uses you,
For their own sake.

Haajirah Assam (11)
Connaught School for Girls

Winter

Winter, winter, snowy winter,
Old people coughing, sitting by the fire.

Ice, ice, slipping ice,
Look at the sky,
Gloomy and dark,
Children wrapped up in the park.

Noisy neighbours,
Creating a nuisance.

Turn up,
Turn up,
Greet the cold,
Whether you're young or old.

Empty trees,
Looking so bare,
The wind roaring,
Like a bear.

River slippery,
All covered with snow,
Bright, powerful glow.

Zainab Hussain (11)
Connaught School for Girls

My Love

When I look into your eyes,
I suddenly grow to your size,
You make me feel,
Like an envelope being sealed,
As a tear drops straight down my eye,
You sigh,
But with happiness,
You are everything I need,
To guide me through this horrible deed,
We both know we can be together,
Indeed forever,
You tell me to never give up,
So I stand up with my head rising up,
No one is better than me,
Or lower than me,
So let's be together,
Because I love you
And you love me.
Love.

Jourdan Roberts (12)
Connaught School for Girls

I Am

I am like a bee,
I can really sting,
I am like a bee,
But I am as small as a ring.

I am as cheery as a hyena,
I tell funny jokes,
I am as cheery as a hyena,
But I am scared of smoke.

I am as brave as a lion,
Can't you see?
But when I'm not myself,
How can I be me?

Nabila Rashid (11)
Connaught School for Girls

Detention

D etention, detention, yeah I just got a detention,
E ating my lunch, then someone threw a punch,
T esting my patience,
E ager to punch,
N ow
T ime to let my anger go,
I n my head, my heart, it is going to come out,
O ut it comes to punch her,
N o I didn't. *Yes! I did, I punched her.*
Great, you know what that means,
Detention!

Riá Lindsay (11)
Connaught School for Girls

Panic

I pulled my duvet, put on my sock,
Looked at my timer and saw 8 o'clock,
Jumped out of bed,
Bumped my head
And turned the key in my lock,
I was leaping stair by stair,
Ran my fingers through my hair,
I was shivering, feeling chilly and cool,
Knowing how late I was going to be for school,
I put on my clothes, packed my bag
And slipped on my mum's TV mag,
I did my hair, raced for the door,
Was I going to make it? I wasn't sure,
I ran to school, reached the gate,
Now knowing that I was late,
I didn't do my homework, it was comprehension,
You know what that means?
Double detention.

Killiesha-Chante Bancroft (11)
Connaught School for Girls

Freedom Is Yours

During the long course of life, it is plain to see,
I was not put on this Earth to please,
To please anyone but myself would be wrong,
My family taught me to be strong.

I don't take life for granted, that just isn't me,
I was never brought up to be naïve,
Live my life to the full, is what I say,
The consequences that may come
May be too much to take.

I'm not old, but I believe I'm wise beyond my years,
No one else my age has cried so many tears,
Tears of joy, tears of pain, tears of misfortune,
Tears for great gain.

I sometimes feel I'm all alone,
No one to love me, no one to hold,
But only then does it hit home,
The love and acceptance must come from within,
You do not know where you're going,
Until you know where you've been,
My family always tell me I was born to be me,
To please anyone else but myself would be wrong,
I now teach myself to be stronger than strong.

It won't take long for me to realise,
That the passion inside me is all full of lies,
No one to hold me when I am down,
No one to turn my frowns around,
Just me and my inner soul waiting to be healed,
All the tears I cry are waiting to be sealed,
To please everyone else but myself would be wrong,
I now teach myself to be stronger than strong.

Sachan Shanli Popo Williams (12)
Connaught School for Girls

Friendship

Friends are forever,
Boys are whatever,
When worse becomes worst,
My girls come first,
Nothing can come between us,
We don't let each other down,
Friends keep your secrets inside of them and don't tell anyone,
We hold our heads up high,
Friendship like ours lasts for eternity,
Our friendship is *perfect!*

Shivani Patel (12)
Connaught School for Girls

Mixed Up

My feelings are mixed up so I don't know what to do,
Feelings so mixed up, they may never be true,
You hurt me bad, you really did,
Some things I know I may never forgive,
But thinking back to times before,
I think I may love you even more,
Everything different but our love remains,
A love that's strong only God can explain.

But that will not help me if God does not speak,
The one thing I need to know our God keeps,
So how am I going to find out what to do?
If I say I don't, but I do still love you,
Trying to hard to put the past behind,
But not one sane reason can I find,
To throw away the love that only God can explain,
Because that feeling of love will always remain.

Will always remain,
I hope will remain,
I know in my heart will always remain,
But one day I know God will explain . . .

Lydia Amartey (14)
Connaught School for Girls

Over You . . .

I'm sitting here going through the poems and I'm feeling very confused,
I'm trying to figure out which one to enter, which one will show
                                                            the abuse,

I can't decide on a specific one so I'm taking a
Stanza from each one,
I have a right to tell people and to let it out in the sun,
This surely will be fun . . .

I want you to know the truth,
But I don't want to tell you 'cause I know I'll look like a fool,
Why I fell for you I'll never know,
Something came to me and just wouldn't go,
God made you, God made me,
God never made 'we' for you and me . . .

I can't lie anymore, I really like you,
I can't get over you, it's way too hard,
I tried to lie about hating you,
But it's gone too far, I just can't get over you . . .

I want something to feel,
Something real to feel,
But what should I feel?
Please tell me what I should feel . . .

You give me butterflies,
When I try to fly high into the sky,
Where in my dreams I can touch you,
Where in my dreams I can hold you,
Where in my dreams I can love you,
I'm scared, just so scared . . .

This is how I felt about you but not anymore 'cause . . .

You were my everything, everything that I wanted,
But now you're nothing to me, nothing to me 'cause you lost me . . .

Ankita Patel (15)
Connaught School for Girls

Oceans Above

Oceans above so loud and clear,
When I'm near you I feel no fear,
A wealth of sea life, some large and some small,
Oh ocean, oh ocean, you have it all.

I put my hand in your crystal-blue waters,
I touch a slippery turtle,
You slide through my fingers so delicately,
Oh ocean, oh ocean, as far as the eye can see.

The wind blows slowly,
While you're still lonely,
Your waves drift softly,
Oh ocean, oh ocean, you move so elegantly.

You glimmer in the sunshine,
You're just so divine,
I watch you in the moonlight,
Oh ocean, oh ocean, I want you to be mine.

Hayley Fitzpatrick (11)
Connaught School for Girls

Because Of You

Because of you,
My heart was broken,
Because of you,
My happiness was stolen.

Because of you,
The only thing left was to die,
Because of you,
I couldn't even bear to look into your eyes.

Because of you,
All the pain I received, after a while, never hurt,
Because of you,
It was all I'd ever felt.

Because of you,
My laughter turned into tears,
Because of you,
Nobody even cares.

Because of you,
My sunshine turned to rain,
Because of you,
My life was not the same . . .

Sahra Siddiqui (13)
Connaught School for Girls

My Eyes

The window's open,
Out pours the unknown,
For everyone to see,
But the gallery is shut and no one is home.

A single glance at the family photo,
A happy family? Who knows?

A kite,
The hand is holding on too tight,
The string might just *s-n-a-p*
It needs to, it wants to be free,
To fly solo in the sky,
Out of the window . . .

A tape measure,
L-o-n-g? Of course,
Simple? Not at all,
From foot to foot it reaches,
Yet twenty planets away,
The sin winds on . . . and on.

The window's closed,
The unknown locked away,
The curtains pulled shut, so no rain gets in,
Time to go to bed,
Once again no one sees.

Rykesha Hudson (15)
Connaught School for Girls

Roses Are Red . . .

Roses are red,
Violets are blue,
Honey is sweet
And so are you.

Daffodils are yellow,
Poppies red,
I lay in bed,
Thinking of you.

Your shimmering blue eyes,
Like a pond of crystals,
I'll bake you a pie,
Full of love and kisses.

Our love is true,
Just like the sky is blue,
A kiss upon a cheek,
From me to you.

Farah Ahmed (12)
Connaught School for Girls

Will I?

The wind whistles through my fingers,
My toes deeply buried in the sand,
Gently the waves lap against my feet,
As I watch the sun set underneath the sea.

Every day they call me horrible names,
Whatever I try to do,
At my new home it's terrifying enough,
But at school and on the streets it's much worse.

Shivering with immense cold inside the water,
My bedraggled hair falling down to my waist,
Salted water feels sticky sweet on my tongue,
With the last rays of sunlight disappearing.

When I came from my country,
They all somehow seemed to know,
That I was the one who was different,
So they wanted to make my life a misery.

Looking at my reflection in the sea,
Only a pair of sunken eyes stare back at me,
Slowly, tears ran down my golden-brown cheeks,
Clearly visible in the moonlight.

Will I ever fit in? Will I ever get a chance?
Will I ever be appreciated for who I am
Or will I have to hide with shame?
Will I?

Saima Undre (11)
Connaught School for Girls

Days

Days, we spend so much time thinking of how bored we are,
But we never stop to think what we could do with it
All our time, wasted on being so negative,
When instead there is so much positive on a plate
Waiting for us
And when we see it,
When we finally see that everything is not so bad,
Something small comes along and we let that
Take away our happiness, our joy,
We allow something so petty, something so insignificant
To wipe the smile off our faces.

When will we wake up and recognise that
Everything we are complaining about,
Doesn't really mean anything at all?
Just look around and see all the people,
With nothing, nothing at all,
Their world's surrounded with sadness and sorrow
And all we can say is 'I'm bored!'
Sad
Isn't it?

Shani-Louise Osei (12)
Connaught School for Girls

Friendship . . .

Friendship is an honour,
Friendship is a gift.

We could be friends,
As long as we live.

Friendship is honoured,
Friendship is gifted.

When we walk,
We're always together.

Friendship is . . .

Friendship is something you honour,
You never know when you could lose it.

Friendship is a gift we could never forget,
So cherish it as carefully as you can.

I'm certain,
We will be
Best friends forever!

Samra Malik (12)
Connaught School for Girls

Maths

Addition and plus - show a bit of determination
And they're no fuss!
Subtraction, minus and take away,
Can make you think for the whole day.

Multiply, times and the letter X -
With a larger number, these can make me vexed,
Division and sharing - with these,
You have to take more care in.

The mode, median and range,
These all are averages
And at times they can be strange,
Diagrams, pie charts and data,
When I look at these, I want to do them later!

Areas, perimeters and 3D shapes,
If you know the formula, it's a piece of cake.

Rounding up, rounding down may sometimes make you frown,
But if you work hard and persevere,
There's not a sum you need to fear!

Sharrell Marshall (11)
Connaught School for Girls

The Only Way

No other way to say it,
I don't know what to do,
I think I've cried forever,
All hope is done and through,
I feel like I just lost you,
Something I never had,
I spent forever wishing,
It nearly drove me mad.

So I'm counting down the minutes,
I'm counting down the days,
I need to get away from you,
I have to find a way.

No other way to say it,
I have to leave you behind,
Moving on, it's not that hard,
Just scared of what I'll find.

Ambia Begum (12)
Elizabeth Garrett Anderson Girls' School

The World

People these days are very aggressive,
Always want revenge but never forgive,
People get killed, beaten and treated horribly,
Who knows when this world will live in harmony?

Everyone should unite and be together,
Because nobody knows if we will live forever,
Why can't we all live in peace?
And when will these troubles cease?

Most people live in fear,
Even some reduced to tears,
Why do people hate each other?
It shouldn't mater what race, religion or colour.

All of us should be treated the same,
Whatever age, birthday or name,
We are all a multicoloured society,
The world is better when there's a variety.

Who cares if you're Caribbean, African, American,
European or Asian,
We will always be one nation.

Chisom Edomobi (14)
Elizabeth Garrett Anderson Girls' School

Spiders

Spiders, oh spiders I hate you so,
Tarantulas and daddy-long-legs, why can't you go?
While I do my homework, I try to think,
Then I see you crawling, I wish I could put you down the sink!
I get a glass to capture you,
But you're just too fast,
The cup slips out of my hand, this fight won't last!
Spiders, oh spiders I hate you so,
Tarantulas and daddy-long-legs, why can't you go?

Torah Louise Browne (12)
Elizabeth Garrett Anderson Girls' School

What Is War?

Why do we go to war?
To kill one another,
To pierce each other's hearts,
To turn a family's life upside down,
To kill.
What do we get out of war?
We win, win what?
In some cases it's freedom,
But at the same time, we are killers.
What does this say to children?
That killing is right.

War is a lot more than toy soldiers.

Elly Savill (12)
Elizabeth Garrett Anderson Girls' School

All The Army Ever Does

All the army ever does,
Is send you to war,
Only because of,
One old man's bore.

Why don't they,
Fight for themselves,
Because that way,
Not as many people would kill themselves.

Instead of one old man's life,
Die many more,
Hundreds of men leave their wives,
Because one old man knows a little more.

Most of these people,
Don't come back,
All they leave,
Is a memory, a tear, a body.

Al Mahdi Ali (13)
Geoffrey Chaucer Technology College

Isn't It Funny?

Isn't it funny you can have so many emotions,
In just one life?
Depression, sadness, happiness, strife,
It's a weird life, it's full of changes,
You never know where you're going to,
Life is full of decisions on the spot,
You have to think what to do,
It's like lions shouting and nagging everywhere you look,
Fashion victims whining, where's your school book?
Changes, colour, my life is turning into a blur,
I'm in a cauldron and the witches are giving me a stir,
My mind is out of *control*,
Huh, a shiver, I'm cold,
I'm in my bedroom,
It's dark, a bit of a gloom,
The blankets are down,
It's 7.20am, I'm late for school,
I don't care,
I start to think about primary,
I wonder if they remember me,
It's funny life, the changes.

Abigail Shadare (11)
Geoffrey Chaucer Technology College

Sports Poem

The football team I like is *Liverpool,*
Because they are the best and they are *cool,*
Liverpool plays like roaring *professionals,*
Because they are better than *Arsenal,*
The way Zabi Alonso shoots the ball, he shoots it like *thunder,*
Everyone screams and says *Wonder Boy.*

Ozden Eratli (12)
Geoffrey Chaucer Technology College

Sea Shows Us How We Are!

When I see the sea,
It reminds me of people,
When I see the sea calm,
It reminds me of people in a good mood,
But when I see the sea waves crash against the rocks,
It reminds me of people with short tempers.

It is horrible when we see the sea crash against the rocks,
That's how some people are.

For we should be like the sea when it is calm,
Then everyone will be happy in a place like the Earth.

Dionisa Hadziu (11)
Mount Carmel Technology College

My Cat

Baby Bubbles is the name of my cat,
She's fluffy and furry and loves the colour black.

She's white all over, pink on her nose
And red and yellow around her toes.

She loves the sun but hates the rain,
Because she knows they are no games to play.

Baby Bubbles loves to dance,
Whenever there's music on, she boogies down,
Taking my hand, spinning around and around.

When I'm in trouble, she always knows
And runs as fast as a cheetah on the go.

She smells as sweet as bee's honey,
She loves to cuddle up to her big blue bunny.

For goodness sake, she's always awake!

Roseanna Barton (12)
Mount Carmel Technology College

Mount Carmel

M is for manners, which are what we're taught in school,
O is for origins, we have different origins in our school,
U is for uniform, to unite we're all together representing
   Mount Carmel,
N is for nervous, especially on our first day of school,
T is for test and teachers, they are the most difficult things in school!

C is for college, one of the next steps in our lives,
A is for assessments and assemblies, both always so long!
R is for registration, great when we have discussions,
M is for music, one of my best subjects,
E is for energy when we run around during break times,
L is for lunchtime when we scream and shout.

Ebony Lartey (12)
Mount Carmel Technology College

We Are All Made In God's Image

God loves us,
Because He made us,
God treasures us,
More than the animals,
God says, 'Don't worry about life,'
Because He's got it under control,
God loves animals too,
Just like me and you,
God is inside me and you,
So praise His holy name,
Even though we hurt Him,
He still loves us and
His love will never let go.

Kenya Mason-Barned (12)
Mount Carmel Technology College

Place Poem

I see the beach, it is crystal-blue like diamonds,
I can hear the sea whilst crashing on the sand,
I'm smelling the salty water,
What I can feel below my feet is little grains of sand,
I am on a beach in Kish Island, Persian Gulf.

Saman Sadri-Shirani (14)
Riverston School

A Place I Went

The station on a very busy day,
Cramped and stuffy.

I see different people from all over the world,
Walking past,
Cars trying to go over the limit,
Traffic building up.

The smell of junk food,
Under the buildings I stand.

This is Victoria Station.

Rashel Ahmed (13)
Riverston School

Cyprus

The countryside makes me alive and energised in the morning,
The wide waves relax my mind,
Behind me I hear the leaves touching each other,
The saltwater relaxes my skin when I touch it,
The sand looks like 24-carat gold,
When the sun touches it,
The old traditional bar plays,
Pop music, rap, filling the air with fast sounds,
Trees next to the bar are growing coconuts,
The tables under a shelter have views of the inviting sea,
This is Cyprus.

Tanju Ozsoykal (13)
Riverston School

The Basement

Widescreen plasma TV, surround sound system,
High bass, HD, MTV Base.

After watching MTV Base,
Laughter, DEF jam, comedy,
DVD.

Popcorn, eating, crunchy, buttery,
Sticky, popcorn tastes good,
The popcorn bowl, plastic, smooth
And smells great.

The swimming pool just outside,
In the sun, glistening, waiting,
For people to get in.

The sauna scorching, gold and wooden,
The Fahrenheit of one hundred degrees,
You could melt like an ice cube in the direct sun.

This is the basement.

Ojerime Ewujowoh (13)
Riverston School

Siren

S creaming sounds in the air,
I nside the shelter fear of death everywhere,
R aging bullets, you want to be aware,
E ngines running like a cruel snare in the sky,
N ever knowing if you're going to say goodbye.

Enoch Babumba (12)
Riverston School

Air Raid

Air raid sounds are overhead,
The sirens make you get out of bed.

The shelter is where everyone goes,
So that no one's shot in rows.

My mum takes us into the underground shelter,
It's crowded with frightened people,
All that is heard is crying and screaming.

When the bombings are over,
We come out of our shelter.

Our house is destroyed,
We have nowhere to live,
Neither do lots of other people.

James Bristow (12)
Riverston School

Yorkshire

The countryside wide and far, small roads,
Close and near,
Dusty winds, fast, swift and cold.

The rough saltwater fragrance up my nose,
The prickly grass touching my hand.

The fields full of wheat,
The rumbling sound of the tractor going past my ear.

The strong smell of the compost on the fields,
The wheat being harvested ready to eat.

This is Yorkshire.

Adeel Hussain (13)
Riverston School

You Only Live Once

The sirens wailing, panic all around,
The distant sound of the Luftwaffe
Engines drawing closer, to find and
Destroy our precious lives, waiting
For the high-pitched scream of falling
Bombs, the crash, as they crumpled a
House to the ground, my family
Fading into a sleepy panic, still
Waiting for the scream overhead,
But did not come, but did not come,
The crash landing very close, the wail
Of ambulances driving me into a
Sleep realm, the door opened to reveal
Utter devastation.

Conor Cooke (12)
Riverston School

Adventure In Germany

On the rich sandy beach,
I was lying in the sand,
I was so hot,
I couldn't get up,
I was dripping in sweat like a wet dog,
As I tried to get on my feet.

On the rich sandy beach,
I was melting in the sand,
I was so hot,
I felt like my skin was cooking,
I walked along the boiling beach,
Into the cold and relaxing sea.

I went so deep,
That the water
Covered
My eyes.

Cameron Steele-Perkins (14)
Riverston School

Air Raid

Snookers flying overhead,
Leaving booming noises behind,
Bodies lying everywhere,
Little children hiding.

Boom! Boom! go the bombs,
Craters left where buildings stood,
Rubble left on the ground below,
When will this war end for good?

Boom! Boom! Another bomb goes off,
Panic in the streets,
People running everywhere,
I'm running for my life.

Enemy soldiers begin to attack,
Anti-aircraft firing too,
We're all under attack, *boom! Boom!*
We're all doomed.

Keegan Tappin (13)
Riverston School

One To Ten

One wicked wizard won the wobbling contest,
Two tight tomatoes told tense tourists to tremble,
Three thunderbolts threatened to thump things,
Four fat fish fabulously flew through the fancy farm,
Five foolish fathers fed foxes fast food,
Six sparrows specialised in spanking special spiders,
Seven salty sprouts spoke speckled Spanish,
Eight acting adults ate advertising aeroplanes,
Nine naked nails naughtily used neck nappies,
Ten technical trees tended to play terrible tennis.

Alexander Shelkoplyas (11)
Riverston School

One Waggily Whale

One waggily whale waded a wet wager,
Two terrible tigers taunted a terrified tarantula,
Three topless toffees tried a tempting turkey,
Four funny fish fiddled about with their fins,
Five foreign fish found a floating foreigner,
Six slithering sea serpents slithered stealthily,
Seven silly sharks splashed stupidly,
Eight extreme elephants entered an elephant elevator,
Nine nutty ninjas nibbled nuts,
Ten twittering tarantulas tried a terrible toffee.

James Whitehead (11)
Riverston School

One Wobbly Wombat

One wobbly wombat wobbled with Willy Wonka,
Two thick toddlers thieved Tesco,
Three thieves stole two tubby turkeys,
Four fat firefighters threw five foolish pheasants,
Five fidgeting freaks flung five fiddly fish,
Six silly sharks shredded some soggy sandwiches,
Seven striking sea serpents sounded silently Spanish,
Eight annoying Eskimos ate eighteen arrogant eagles,
Nine nibbling natterjacks nibbled ninety nuts,
Ten tumbling tigers topped ten Tesco trolleys.

Joshua Stephens (12)
Riverston School

1-10 Poem

One wobbly whale watched a walrus wobble,
Two tiny thick thieves thieved Tesco,
Three things foolishly fell through four fat turkeys,
Four foreign freaky fat firefighters thickly threw four foot full
Foolish fancy fireworks fiercely fast,
Five fiddly figs fell flat on the floor,
Six superstars sucked at some spitting snakes' skin,
Seven silly stupid sea surfers surfed some seas,
Eight annoying arrogant atom ants ate apples at Alaska,
Nine nutty ninjas nibbled ninety nuts,
Ten tiny tumbling towers tumbled.

Dennie Aris (11)
Riverston School

Football Mayhem

One waggly Wayne wobbled wackily to the hospital,
Two topping Totis tackled Thierry,
Three topless turkeys belched the Tangos,
Four fierce men fought on the frozen field,
Five ferocious females failed to score a goal,
Six superstars signed a contract to Sainbury's,
Seven stupid superstars sneaked silently to Somerfield,
Eight athletic all-stars acted the 'All-Stars' talent show,
Nine naughty natterjacks nibbled Nathan,
Ten timeless tigers told Tina off.

Pavan Patel (12)
Riverston School

Alone

High or low,
Big or small,
He is up there. Alone.
No one to speak to. No one to be comforted by,
Just alone,
Ropes hanging from this brave and mighty body,
To keep his life like a guardian angel, standing,
Waiting.
He's up there,
With no one,
Alone,
All protection is poor,
Only to rely on crampons, ropes
And a white helmet,
Glistening in the dangerous environment of nothing,
Nothing but nature,
To take its place,
Where's he going? Why's he doing it?
Only he knows,
There's no one to tell,
Alone, in his own world, alone.

Henry Nicholson (13)
Riverston School

My Sonnet

This heart is beating at a quickened pace,
Love wrapped around me like a veil of lace,
I once was alone then soon you found me,
When dreaming of love, it's you that I see.

Fluttering wildly I'm tied up in strings,
Love for my partner I show with this ring,
The aisle is looming, my words have run dry,
My love stands before me with passionate eyes.

The better side of me, my other half,
He is devoted and he makes me laugh,
Tender and caring, all of the above,
Marvellous feelings of being in love.

But that was before and now I'm alone,
To unfaithful lovers it seems I am prone.

Rebecca Masters (16)
Riverston School

An Ancient Treasure

She is said to be an ancient treasure,
Visiting her is said to be a pleasure,
That's *Istanbul*.

The tip of the mosques scraping the sky,
The Bosphorus, right there it lies,
That's Istanbul.

Her former name, Constantinople,
Her present name, Istanbul,
That's Istanbul.

She holds the world's expensive jewel and gem,
People gather from the world to catch a glimpse of them,
That's Istanbul.

Topkapi, Sultan, they are all the same,
Spectacular scenes that have traditional names,
That's Istanbul.

She holds the gateway between Europe and Asia,
That's Istanbul!

Can Yavuzarslan (13)
Riverston School

A Cat's View Of Life

Hello? Hello?
I'm hungry,
Give me food,
Acknowledge me,
Give me attention,
Oh well I better get up,
Owwww my legs,
Hello I'm up!
Ah . . . I know how to get them to give me attention,
Miaow! Miaow! Miaow!
Oh well back to sleep.
Zzzzzzz.

James Ogden (13)
Riverston School

Events In Our Country

Where is the love, the peace and tranquillity?
The world is driven by hostility,
The message is lucid, spread peace and love,
Don't look downwards but to the skies above.

Many are blinded by greed and ambition,
Terrorism is cruel and partner to suspicion,
Politicians bickering about improvement,
If they united they could be a movement.

Who really cares above the environment's needs?
Cutting down trees and planting a few seeds?
Does Mr Blair need the sack or are people just bored?
Will the polar ice caps ever be thawed?

Is it true we are all going the wrong way?
The time will come when we are going to pay.

Humza Farooqui (15)
Riverston School

Human Mixture

Like Beethoven, you move me from one
rhythm to another.
Black notes, my tears are released.
Like his greatest hits.
White notes, my body is trampled on.
Like his unbreakable song.
Swirl and whirl them both together,
What do you get?
A painting by Picasso . . .
The Mona Lisa perhaps?
Alone, deserted, trapped -
In the forest and trees behind her,
I imagine myself swinging on the trees,
the pollen and scent of the flowers,
attacking my nose.
Einstein, a great genius,
Unlike the likes of yourself.
Inventor of great things - or what
eyes see today and those
which people seem to miss.
Like you miss me, myself, my feelings,
My pain, my hurt . . .

Silva Gashi (16)
St Anne's Catholic High School for Girls, Palmers Green

Mum

My mum is the most
Important woman in my life,
She helps me with my homework,
When I get stuck,
My mum calms me down when I get angry,
My mum loves me and I love her too,
My mum, my mum, my ever so gorgeous mum,
The number one woman in my life,
Number 1, not 2 or 3,
My mum does what she can to help me when I mess up,
I really do mess up a lot,
If I could give an award,
For the best woman in my life,
It would go to my mum!

Shaquelle Hendricks (11)
St Joseph's Academy for Boys, Blackheath

Sky Is Dark

Sky is dark but not scary,
Sky is full of stars,
But only one moon,
I look at the sky,
There is nothing flying,
Except a moon and a bunch of stars,
All I see is black as coal,
I look again, I see an aeroplane,
Which reminds me of my cousin going on an aeroplane,
Sky looks beautiful with all the beautiful colours,
Like yellow for stars and moon
And blue and red,
From the aeroplanes.

Chandraruban Sarveswaran (11)
St Joseph's Academy for Boys, Blackheath

Starlight Mum

Starlight Mum,
Who I owe my life,
If not for her,
I wouldn't be.

Starlight Mum,
My twinkle in the sky,
The heart I can share,
With memories from
The past,
Never ever to be lost.

Starlight Mum,
How I love her,
So much
Our love is gone
Gone.

Starlight Mum,
Who brought me here,
With a heart of gold.

Oh Starlight Mum,
Please don't go.

Dekota Navaroa
St Joseph's Academy for Boys, Blackheath

I Wonder

I wonder when the sun will shine
I wonder when they will stop the crime.

I wonder when I'll get my cat,
I wonder if it will eat the rat.

I wonder if I'll learn to fly,
Above the rainbow, above the sky.

I wonder when there will be peace divine,
Throughout the nations, across the world.

I wonder when we shall all change,
Learn to be nice and respect.

I wonder . . .

Leslie Sackey (11)
St Joseph's College, Beulah Hill

Monster

In the darkness of the night,
He slinks rough corners dark and tight,
He's the creature of your nightmares,
With a heart of steel and eyes of stone,
Destruction is his game,
Death is his name.

Daniel Goudie (12)
St Joseph's College, Beulah Hill

Monkey World

The monkeys run the shops and schools,
They run the fire department,
Run the hospital and police,
The theatre and tailors.

They act and sing and dance about,
The carnivals are crazy,
Their houses are filled with monkey bars,
The beds and sheets are messy.

No fried chicken or burgers or crap,
Banana milkshakes are popular,
The trousers have holes for tails,
Their cars are smaller than ours.

Imagine the banana prices!

Paul Klein (12)
St Joseph's College, Beulah Hill

Planet Football

Lampard, Terry and Wayne Roo',
Playing for their club, country, and planet too,
Earth vs Mars, March 31st,
People watching from their aircraft.

How big is the stadium?
Ten of Wembley,
Earth scores,
The crowd cheers with glee.

Computerised commentators,
They all shout goal,
Hundreds of languages,
Martian, Venution, and Plutonium.

Why Terry, Rooney and Frank Lampard?
Because life is endless,
Just like a red card.

Jake Fryer (12)
St Joseph's College, Beulah Hill

The Year 4000

The year 4000 is very bright,
With simulated day and simulated night,
The sun and the moon are both robots,
Imitating those poor, sweet baby tots.

Technology and transport so improved,
You could shoot off in a second without knowing you have moved,
The sky is not blue but it is boggy green,
It's in high definition like a television screen.

For some strange reason the trees don't grow
And the birds don't fly,
Maybe there is a logical reason or they might be just shy,
There is a lot of technical stuff everywhere in sight,
Because the year 4000 is very bright.

Joe Rose (12)
St Joseph's College, Beulah Hill

Solar System Planet Three

(Sol 3) Mysteries

Beautiful are the strong fragrances of scented flowers,
Graceful is the traditional and picturesque landscapes,
Cheerful are the residents and inhabitants of the Earth and
Peaceful are the races of nations that were once at war or sinful.

Joyful is the man-made instruments used by the people,
Hopeful are the tranquil facts of the spherical world,
Plentiful is the enriched ripened fruit that cover the planet,
Playful is the amazing and talented animals that roam
the land and sea.

P eople whose intellects are so expanded they have
Written and acted as a race in the union of life,
L uminescence is the world of new as new technology is born
Any illness is a joke among friends as all diseases were wiped out
A thousand years ago,
N atural animals have been isolated to the continent America and
marine life still owns the waters.
E ducation has been so advanced they teach you GCSE standard
Year 6 and KS3 is taught in Year 1 and 2.
T errestrial life is reborn with different races of aliens
Living among us.

This is a Utopian view of the future,
'Dystopian' as a word is used as an insult
And people duly use it to teach to their siblings,
To even see the word 'dystopia' in the year 4000 can get you
punished.

Dwayne Spiteri (12)
St Joseph's College, Beulah Hill

From The Future

A message of what it's like from the future,
Up in the sky, looking down on people,
What I want I just say and it's there,
The robots do what I want them to,
I'm so powerful, so people beware,
I am the leader of Britain, I'm as rich as a person can be,
I don't really care about my people,
But they'll never be richer than me.

I'm in my room watching telly, make a billion every day,
I take all the people's money,
Cos people will do what I say,
I am the guy off the advert, from the company that
                              takes all your cash,
You don't know our stuff is useless,
But we make trillions from our trash.

Down on the ground looking upwards,
Wishing I could be like them,
I make just enough to stay living,
It's a struggle every day,
I'm Debbie from the doctors, I help people every day,
I'm more important than half the rich ones,
But do they care about me?

I'm on the street getting beaten,
By the police who hate people like me,
Just because I don't work and sit here all day,
They think my pain is funny,
I'm Kevin who doesn't do much,
Just hope to get a bit of cash each day,
I'm not all rich and famous,
I am the lowest degree.

Tom McManamon (12)
St Joseph's College, Beulah Hill

My Odyssey Poem

I started travelling in 2012,
Surfing through the universe
And falling through time,
My ship is so fantastic,
Nebula-powered
And radiation-proof.

Five years have past
And what have I seen,
Human evolution
And an alien war,
Us humans won
And peace was restored,
Now to start my journey over again.

In a new galaxy,
Nothing's the same,
All planets are run by dictatorship
And clearly you can see,
It's a dystopia.
There is no peace,
Just destruction,
If I get to close, I'd be vaporised.

As I come to the end,
How do I feel?
Happy and sad,
The terror I've seen . . .
Happily I return
Back to my home,
Seeing my family
And a proper night's rest.

Antony Chapman (12)
St Joseph's College, Beulah Hill

In The Future

In 1000 years we see the future,
Flying cars, no more losers,
We see robots and machines,
Teleporters, robot teachers, robots who clean.

Hopefully people will see,
That we should not harm nature and trees,
No wars and fights, people who might,
Have nations' good at first sight.

Europe, Asia comes together,
Africa, America at peace with each other,
All the nations along with Austria,
Come together pure as a feather.

Also in the future,
News and corporations,
New technology,
Maybe new nations.

In the future,
New governments,
New laws and taxes,
Ways of contacting,
Better than faxes.

Spinning channels,
On TV,
Walking on air,
We will see.

So I feel
A Utopian view,
Of the future, it seems cool.

Onome Oyibo (12)
St Joseph's College, Beulah Hill

A Diamond Ring

A diamond ring was once swept onto a shore,
Not on the headland but quite near the moor,
The villagers squealed and shouted in awe -
Though not one knew what they had saw!

Meanwhile the desperate owner searched far and wide,
For her diamond ring with the glittering side,
Though she knew it had long been swept away by the waves,
Its memory was as sharp as knives.

The villagers ran to the edge of their land,
Shouting and playing with a band,
Keeping in time with the mellow beat,
They attracted many a sweet . . .

The ever-despairing woman,
Heard this noise and came to them
And asked what was going on!
She did not realise until she saw . . .
The glittering side of her diamond ring!

That was the tale of a diamond ring,
Whenever you have time -
Remember this as a way of peace in mind . . .

Monica Di Carlo (12)
St Paul's Academy, Wickham Lane

Like An Angel

I sit in my room here,
It is dim, dark, cold,
I stare at the room wall,
Again and again, always.

Nothing makes any sense here,
It is really sorrowful,
There is no goal, no escape given,
In the dismal loneliness.

However then, you, came into my life,
As an angel for a child,
You wanted to return joy to me,
But whether this really is true.

However slowly, I noticed your seriousness,
You were so dear to me,
You ever were like no one before,
My heart brought me to you.

You taught me the life
With patience and time,
You always took me as I am,
I was ready.

Now, we sit together in the room,
So brightly, so shining, you are mine,
I will always hold your hand,
From now on, I will be happy!

Justina Ayowunmi Adu (15)
St Paul's Academy, Wickham Lane

My Free Soul

I am the beauty of my creation,
The one and only queen to my kingdom,
I live the truth and only the truth,
No more lies and no more pain.

I lay beneath my twitching red roses,
I call upon the almighty king,
I believe in who I am,
No more lies and no more pain.

I plucked my soul out of its secret place
And held it to the mirror of my eye,
To see it like a star against the sky,
No more lies and no more pain.

I know my soul,
Wherever I go I will always have my soul,
A spark of passion shining on my face,
No more lies and no more pain.

Carry me out to the ocean where my drifting soul flows free,
Guide it to a distant land that only my mind can see,
There I shall paint a great portrait of what my world should be,
No more lies and no more pain.

Natasha Byaruhanga (12)
St Paul's Academy, Wickham Lane

Homework!

I get homework every day,
It's not fair, I want to play,
So when the teacher goes to say,
'Sorry Jo, your homework's late!'

I go mad, I lose my head,
I make enough noise to wake the dead,
It's all because of what the teacher said,
This is why it's homework I dread.

Joanna Williams (12)
St Paul's Academy, Wickham Lane

What If . . .

What if the sky was yellow
    And dogs were pink?
What if the grass was purple
    And pigs could fly?
What if dinosaurs could talk
    And ships could do stunts?
What if peas were full of sugar
    And eggs laid chickens?
What if rats chased cats
    And grasshoppers were smart?
What if mothers were fat
    And babies ruled the Earth?
What if a bomber thought people
    And computers were smarter than humans?
What if your brain was
    Ready for you to look forward in life?

Alex Conteh
St Paul's Academy, Wickham Lane

My Wonderful World

I dream in a world
A world of my own
No one else, me on my own.

I live in a dreamland where no one dreams,
I sleep on a soft cloud,
But when it rains, it's really loud.

I can hear lightning,
The way it's fighting the wind.

Andrea Smith (11)
St Paul's Academy, Wickham Lane

The Bully

At 3.15 I wait outside the school gate,
I'll watch the other children rush by,
But there will be one filled with hate.

The other cars will start their engines
And people will make their way home,
But me, just me,
Will be left alone . . .

I heard footsteps behind my back,
They were just footsteps,
But I was scared,
They were loud and scary, my throat went hairy,
But I knew no one else was there.

I turned around and with great surprise,
The bully arose; I closed my eyes,
I felt pain all over again,
A car pulled by the road,
The bully went into running mode,
I guess the bully had a fright,
He ran and ran until out of sight.

It was my mum,
She was late,
While she was in a comfy car,
I was roughed up like a plate.

'What happened? What's wrong?'
She glared at me in fright,
'We need to get home quickly,
Tell me what happened, *now!*
Are you alright?'

When we got home,
She quickly wiped my scars and cuts,
Then she gave me plasters,
To cover all of them up.

My mum gave me courage,
To stand up to the bully,
Really to show him
He's just a big wally.

So when it's 3.15pm
And I wait outside the school gate,
Do you still remember the one person filled with hate?

Now it's time to show what I can really do,
I may not be able to give him lots of pain,
I may not be able to kick all over again,
But I do have a mouth which I use at this place
And you know what I'll tell him right in his face!

You may think you're really tough,
You may think you're strong and rough,
Everyone knows everyone has a weak point,
But I figured out the weak point.

Whatever the day you give people pain,
No, it's not right
And that gives him a fright,
Just then a car pulled up by the road,
Yet again he goes into running mode,
But I know that gave him a fright,
So he will never mess with me any day or night!

Nicole Omotoye (11)
St Paul's Academy, Wickham Lane

Untitled

I run and run
No one's there
I look behind me
Still no one there
But in my head
I hear them shouting and jeering
I see no one there
'Where are they?' I'm saying
Then I see them looking at me
Through the light glaring at me, just fixed
Ready to start at me
I'm thinking, *why aren't they starting on me?*
Why! I just want it over and
Done with then I can go
But still they don't come
I have this sudden urge to
Shout, *so come on then,*
Take your best shot,
But they just stand there,
Looking at me and smiling,
Then they just . . .

Gbemi Falalde (12)
St Paul's Academy, Wickham Lane

I Hate This School So Much

I hate this school,
School hates me,
Some teachers are nice, some teachers are cruel,
But the worst thing of all, there is nothing to do,
I hate this school,
School hates me,
Every time something happens they blame it on me,
You start to panic and don't know what to do,
I hate this school,
School hates me,
You have one chance to explain yourself,
But as you do the teachers say they don't care,
All they only want to hear is what they want to hear,
Not even what the children have got to say,
I hate this school,
School hates me,
They say this school is fair to the children,
But that is a lie, it cannot be denied,
You try to explain yourself, then they say, 'Stop being rude.'
You start to get angry and in a very bad mood,
I hate this school,
School hates me,
They think you're lying, you know it's not true,
At the end of the day you end up in the BMU,
That is why I hate this school.

Amira Ngwana (14)
St Paul's Academy, Wickham Lane

Love

Love is a blessing,
Love is forever.

Love drives you insane,
Love is a weapon.

Love is a gift,
Love is an angel.

Love is the slowest form of suicide.

Love starts with a smile,
Grows with a kiss and ends with a tear.

Love is the best experience,
Love comes swiftly by but never leaves.

Love freezes time,
Love protects you.

Love blinds you,
Love taunts you.

Love protects you,
Love taunts you.

Love is a mental illness,
Love is a virus,
Love imprisons your sense of right and wrong.

Love completes you,
Love conquers all,
Love is precious.

Love is precious,
Love is beautiful,
Love is God's purpose.

Love is a disease,
Love is a drug,
Love causes changes.

Love is death in disguise . . .

Love is God's purpose.

Sabrina Bhola (15)
Virgo Fidelis School

Gun Crime

Gun crime is wrong and should be stopped.
If you carry a weapon, you're likely to be shot.
Unexpectedly you'll get attacked across the road,
People saw what happened but never told,
Rushed to the hospital with little life left,
Doctors around trying to do their best,
Family in the waiting room pouring out tears,
Mum's praying and praying with so much fear,
Finally the news comes, the bullet pierced through the heart,
Dad, speechless, he doesn't know where to start,
'This can't be true,' Mum said and said,
Dad looks through the room window, 'Dear Bobby's dead!
Who can do this to my innocent son?'
He was laughing yesterday but now he's gone,
Was he fighting with the criminals and then he took out his gun
Or was the criminal stupid and did it for fun?
Preparing for the funeral, what a sad day,
'I told him not to go to the shop but he always had his way!'
Don't be dumb, trash the gun!
Don't be tense, use your sense!

Olivia Okunrinkoya (13)
Virgo Fidelis School

Bullying

It's the end of school now,
I have to get away but how?
I walk briskly towards the gate,
I stand there awaiting my fate.

I'm battered to the ground,
Pain strikes in my head like a screaming sound,
My glasses get smashed,
My head is thrashed.

My legs and arms bleeding,
I cry with all my might pleading,
My body whipped,
My clothes ripped.

They laugh with pleasure,
Stealing all my treasure,
My money stolen,
My body swollen.

They leave me to lie,
I stay there and cry,
Dreading tomorrow in vain,
As they will be back tomorrow again.

Kauser Ismailjee (12)
Walthamstow School for Girls

Love Is . . .

Love is the greatest feeling,
Love is like a play,
Love is what I feel for you,
Each and every day,
Love is like a smile,
Love is like a song,
Love is a great emotion,
That keeps us going strong,
I love you with my heart,
My body and my soul,
I love the way I keep loving you,
Like a love I can't control,
So remember when your eyes meet mine,
I love you with all my heart
And I have poured my entire soul into you,
Right from the very start,
That's what my love is . . .

Momopeda Alabi (11)
Walthamstow School for Girls

Love Is A Sickness

We were all put on this world for a reason,
Whatever that reason may be,
I'm sitting here loving and longing,
Loving and longing for thee.

Love is a sickness, not a feeling,
A sickness we can't deny,
Something I do know is that I will love thee until I die.

Another thing I do stress is that
Love will open another door,
For when I am beyond the grave
I will love thee even more!

Charlie Blair (11)
Walthamstow School for Girls

Memorise

From summer's breeze
To
Winters so wet.

From stars that shine
To
Planets so dull.

From blossoming trees
To
Dry, crisp leaves.

From moonlight roofs
To
Blazing hot sun.

From dreamsome wishes
To
Minor little memories.

Jaisea Khaled (11)
Walthamstow School for Girls

In The Springtime

The flowers all bloom and the birds all sing
And animals come out from hibernating,
The gloom and the clouds all fly away
And the sun comes up and shines all day.

Newborn young are always born
And hence a new generation will form,
Everyone's heart is filled with glee
And that is why everyone is happy you see.

Boys and girls play together as one
And everyone seems to be having fun,
Friends and foes forgive and forget
And the punters in the pub make one last bet.

The trees come to life and the grass grows long
And everyone feels like singing a song,
No one has the time to feel low
And all of this happens in the springtime, you know.

Hannah Barrick (14)
Walthamstow School for Girls

Cherry Blossom Trees

Blooming on bare leaf trees,
Are little, tiny, pink cherry blossoms for me,
Now that the winter snow had gone,
The baby blue sky and the sun shone,
The perfect petals peeping through,
Honeysuckle and lavender perfume,
Give the angels back their wings
And risk the loss of everything,
Cherry blossoms are blooming!

A white dove on top of a hill,
Gliding down or standing still,
The gentle breeze slapping our faces,
Cherry blossoms have bloomed!

Iram Mukadam (11)
Walthamstow School for Girls

Bored

I'm bored, I've got nothing to do,
I don't fancy sitting down and watching 'Doctor Who'.
What's the point of going out - it's absolutely pouring down,
Hmm, on TV, there's a clown,
Nah, too stupid and silly for me,
Oh, look over there, a rusty old key,
What does it unlock?
Tick-tock, tick-tock,
Something weird's happening here,
There's something near . . .
Wow, a chest has appeared from nowhere!
Something's blowing my hair . . .
Let's unlock the chest,
I'm breathless, I need to rest,
No, not now, let's have some action!
I'll open the chest just a fraction,
Oooh, spooky, some eyes peering out,
Hands, ready to give me a clout!
Oooh, no, heeelllp, don't take meee!

Rebecca Claydon (11)
Walthamstow School for Girls

Winter

Wind blows everybody goes,
Snow falls winter comes,
Nobody here except for me and you,
They leave us all alone,
Just me and you now,
What shall we do?
It's all covered in snow,
We can't see a thing,
Everything's disappeared,
But *me* and *you!*

Aaishah Rehman (11)
Walthamstow School for Girls

Are You Mine?

As I wake up, I see
You my love, fading away from me,
I run closer and closer to you thinking -
You're mine.
I approach you thinking of a cunning speech or line,
Every time I take one step forward,
You take one step, one step back!
I threw my life away thinking you were all that,
I should have listened to my parents and my peers,
It would have wiped away all my tears.
I guess my planned life story,
Just wasn't in my fate,
You were humiliated, I was offended,
My heart doesn't need a plaster,
It needs to be mended,
I craved over you!
I worshipped you,
You were meant to be mine,
But this time I couldn't take it,
You had cross the line,
So . . . are you mine?

Ayisha Ahmed (11)
Walthamstow School for Girls

Sun

Sun is shiny, sun is good,
Sun is yellow, sun is hot.

Sun is shining everywhere,
People running in underwear.

Sun is really, really hot,
People hate it (not, not, not!)

Look at the people in other seasons,
They're all so sad with feathery coats,
Because there's no meadows.

Odeta Bendoriute (11)
Walthamstow School for Girls

The Fox - Haiku

The fox has a coat
It's red, silky and shining
It's blazing all night.

Kelsey Boatswain-Medlar (12)
Walthamstow School for Girls

The World Is Ours

You hear on the news,
About war and destruction,
You see the fear in people's eyes,
Running from danger, trying to hide.

No matter where they run,
Nor where they hide,
Innocent people,
Are going to die.

Let there be a change,
Let there be a difference,
Let us stay alive,
We can make the difference.

We can change our lives,
We are the next generation,
We shall make a difference,
This is *our* world!

Nadia Yousuf (12)
Walthamstow School for Girls

Boring, Boring, Boring . . .

There's nothing left for me to do,
I'm bored with them,
I'm bored with you,
I'm bored with staying in my room,
I'm bored with going shopping too,
I'm bored with sleep,
I'm bored in bed,
I'm bored with all the food I'm fed,
I'm bored out of my boring head,
I feel as if I'm boring dead,
I'm bored with clouds,
I'm bored with rain,
I'm bored with my computer game,
I'm bored with everything that's the same,
I'm bored with being bored again,
I'm bored with writing boring rhymes,
About my boring, boring times
And so I'll finish being bored,
Let me rest until I'm . . .
Bored again!

Azraa Mehtar (11)
Walthamstow School for Girls

Everlasting Love

My boyfriend's eyes shimmer in the golden moonlight,
His teeth are as white as shiny pearls,
His lips are bold and his smile is bright,
His hair is dark with thick, glossy, black curls.

Your skin is soft, clean and pure,
You always put beautiful smiles on people's faces,
Whenever I'm down you always have the best cure
And you whisk me away to exotic places.

Your voice is gentle and soft when you speak,
Whenever I need you, you're never far,
I have known you for months, days and weeks,
You're always there for me, you are a superstar.

You are the most wonderful person that I have ever known,
I love you with all my heart and never want to let you go,
I know that you love me and care from what you have shown,
I believe that you feel the same way too,
So never let me go.

I know you love me to the core
And I will love you for evermore.

Catherine Sienkiewicz (15)
Walthamstow School for Girls

Untitled

Your eyes are as bright and vibrant as the sun,
You are as hot as Las Vegas weather,
When I'm with you we have plenty of fun
And I'm in Heaven when we are together.

When I am in need you are always there for me,
You are full of life and never let me down,
You look after me and care a lot about me,
You're kind and generous and never frown.

My life with you is never boring,
Your glamorous skin is spotless and pure,
You are adventurous and exciting
And you are the only one for me.

My life wouldn't be the same without you,
No matter what I will still love you.

Rutendo Muzambi (14)
Walthamstow School for Girls

George, Lennie And Others

Two guys on a journey,
One big, one small, George and Lennie,
Out to get a job, together they were,
Working hard on the ranch, staying away from *her*.

Curley's wife, the source of trouble,
Moving around the guys in a floating bubble,
Lonely, hurt, wanting someone to talk to,
Hating her husband, even though *he* knew.

Curley, the man with the 'glove full of Vaseline,'
Waving his fist at people - this is how he was seen,
Ready for a punch up, he thought he was it,
But when Lennie got to him, boy did he go into a fit.

Lennie, with the mind of a child,
Did silly things and acted wild,
He didn't mean to kill the woman, nor the pup,
He lacked common sense and good luck.

Along with the others, there's 'the man' - everyone respected him,
He was tall and cool, his name's Slim,
He understood George unlike anyone else you know
And treated everyone equally, not looking at people as 'high'
and 'low'.

Candy, the old guy has only one hand,
He joins in with the two guys in planning to get land,
Adoring his old dog and reluctant to shoot it,
His dreams were to come true, his candle had been lit.

As everything goes wrong and dreams are trampled upon,
George must go on and wake to a lonely dawn,
Life must go on for him, like it must for you and I,
Read 'Of Mice and Men' it's a good book and this is no lie.

Saneaah Aishah Dhorat (15)
Walthamstow School for Girls

An Ode To Friends

This is a simple poem,
Dedicated to my friends,
Whenever I seem to slip up,
They pick me up again.

Whenever I need someone's help,
They're there for me when I call
And always and forever I know,
They'll catch me when I fall.

I know I'm not amazing,
Or a brilliantly clever friend,
But I just wanted you all to know,
I'm there for you to the end.

So if you feel you need a friend,
Or a 'pick-me up' if you fall,
Don't call me, I'll already be there,
Solid as a wall.

Carel Bennett Calaguas (15)
Walthamstow School for Girls

Newborn Foal

A newborn foal staggers
To his feet seeing, breathing, smelling
His new world,
He relies on his mother's nurture, love,
Care, young, vulnerable, fragile, delicate, love and
Protection,
My eyes see all these,
No,
My eyes see a stunning stallion strong,
Powerful, athletic,
I did see a newborn foal,
Now I see a
Strong stallion
Embracing his new world!

Olivia Capell (11)
Walthamstow School for Girls

I Miss You Grandad

I miss your warm cuddles,
When I'm feeling blue,
I cry the size of puddles,
Because I miss you.

I miss your lovely smile,
When I enter the door,
It's something I'll always walk a mile for,
Because I miss you.

I miss the gentle hand,
That holds me tight when I skip down the way,
It makes me feel safe throughout the day,
Because I miss you.

I miss the goodnight kiss you always gave,
You tucked me up cosily,
While I slept dozily,
Because I miss you.

But now you're away
And safe in the sky,
Watching over me,
Like you didn't die.

All I know now,
Is that you are fine
And you'll always be mine
And I really truly miss you.

Christie Ferrari (13)
Walthamstow School for Girls

Young Writers - 2007: A Poetry Odyssey London

Savage Cat

Mum always says, 'Feed the cat, darling, feed the cat,'
But I don't want to feed a ginger old kitten,
He claws me a lot, but I don't care,
My dream cat looks savage and bitten,
With a devilish grin and a kink in his ear
And people from around, it's him they fear,
He has a flickering tongue and big sharp claws,
A ragged old tail and ragged old paws,
He stands by my side, ready to attack at my command
But be a ginger old kitten? He just can't!

He sneaks into the house and claws the chairs,
He rips down curtains and licks the stairs,
The vegetables get shredded and the cheese gets mauled,
Everyone's fainted or appalled,
Mum screams louder, Dad runs far,
Police lock suspects behind the bars,
They go to bed, thinking, *what a day!*
Then Wolf comes in and makes them pay!
For my enemies get slashed and my friends go free,
Be warned, reader, stay on the right side of me!
Better give me credit, or else, the cheese gets it!

Jordan Trent (11)
Walthamstow School for Girls

Parrots

Beautiful parrots, feathers so neat,
Copying whatever you say sounding so sweet,
Nearly all green there are different ones,
I love them so much I'll have tonnes.

Colourful parrots so pretty
And when they fly away it's such a pity,
Trapped in a cage it doesn't like to be,
So let it out, so it can be free.

Let them run, let them glide,
Let them move side to side,
Let them free,
Let the beautiful parrots glee!

Tayibah Taj (11)
Walthamstow School for Girls

School's Great!

School's great sometimes,
Because there's hardly any crimes.

Play times can sometimes be a pain,
When it starts to rain.

Some lessons are fun,
Although I wish they'd be done.

I like break,
It makes me stay awake.

But out of all I'll tell you what,
Going home beats the lot!

Rabiah Hussain (11)
Walthamstow School for Girls

Life's Colour!

The forest is green,
It makes a beautiful country scene,
Each branch holds an exotic fruit hanging down,
With dusty twigs from gold to brown.

The sky is blue,
Too good to be true,
It awakens as it brings us storm,
With water dripping in rain form.

The flower smell,
The bluebell,
Petals and scent,
All bluebells there to be meant.

The sun orange and bright,
Its birth is to give us light,
Round and circles of hot,
The forest, sky, flowers, sun therefore the whole lot!

Madeeha Hussain (12)
Walthamstow School for Girls

Invasion

My ears hurt from the wind whistling all around me,
It was the only sign of life; dust and destruction was all I could see,
The land was flat now; all life had been destroyed,
Maybe the wind was telling me something, or was I
                                just being paranoid?
There was a deathly stillness everywhere,
How many lives had been claimed, was it worth it?
Is wasn't fair!

My eyes could see nothing but rubble all around,
Skeletal vehicles and victims piled in a mound,
The remains of the house, curtains torn and bloodstained,
The land was so dry and empty of life, it hadn't even rained.

Maybe this land was once corrupted,
Perhaps that is why anger, war and death erupted,
Then, beneath the destruction lay a face,
Half smiling, the other half burnt,
Was this the way you treat someone, for the 'lesson to be learnt'?
Was this how it worked? Led by corruption,
And then victims to pay?
This goes on all over the world, day after day,
It seems the sun doesn't even shine here,
There was nothing but silence, and a sense of fear.

These were the innocent victims, who paid the price
And for their countries and leaders become the sacrifice,
For the survivors there was anger and hate,
Too many lives had been lost, there's no point apologising,
It's too late!
This war will go on, it isn't over yet
And it won't be, because the victims won't forget,
What they went through and revenge has to be met.

Asiya Tanya Tayyib (17)
William Morris Academy

The Real Me

The real me is looking for answers,
The real me is wondering why things happen,
The real me wants to break down and cry,
The real me hates everyone for not realising sooner,
The real me wants to be locked away with nothing but
                                    a pen and paper,
The real me says she is ready to be shown but is far
                        too sceptical to follow through,
The real me is tired of hiding,
The real me wants to shine and be loved,
The real me never wanted to be so shy,
The real me is half broken due to misplaced trust,
The real me is searching for that somebody,
Never realising that *he* has always been there,
The real me is too scared to reach out and touch his hand,
The real me doesn't want to be wrong,
The real me can't take another disappointment,
The real me doesn't reach out,
The real me becomes too weak to look for answers,
The real me no longer cares why things happen,
The real me can't be bothered to break down and cry,
The real me forgives everyone for not realising sooner,
The real me no longer wants to be locked away,
She has no need for the pen and paper,
The real me can't be shown, scepticism has
                        become too overpowering,
The real me is now content with hiding,
The real me doesn't want to shine and be loved,
The real me likes being shy,
The real me is finally broken due to misplaced trust,
The real me has stopped searching and now realises
He was always there,
The real me can no longer be scared to reach out
And touch his hand because the real me is dead.

Lisa-Claire Peynado (17)
William Morris Academy